Ellen Stern has dedicated herself to improving not only her health but that of the whole American public who are not aware that they are all dying of heart disease, diabetes, and cancer. If you follow Ms. Stern's good advice, you can not only lower the risk factors for these devastating diseases, but also enjoy a delicious new experience in eating. You will not only lose your fatigue and feel great, but you will probably save enough in food costs to have a free vacation each year.

—Nathan Pritikin

THE
GOOD
HEART
DIET
COOK
BOOK

THE
GOOD
HEART
DIET
COOK
BOOK

Ellen Stern and Jonathan Michaels

Foreword by Siegfried J. Kra, M.D.
Yale School of Medicine

New Haven and New York
Ticknor & Fields
1982

Library of Congress Cataloging in Publication Data
Stern, Ellen Stock.
    The good heart diet cookbook.

    Includes index.
     1. Heart — Diseases — Diet Therapy — Recipes.
2. Low-cholesterol diet — Recipes. I. Michaels, Jonathan. II. Title.
RC684.D5S84   641.5'6311   81-8938
ISBN 0-89919-053-7   AACR2

Designed by Samuel N. Antupit
Printed in the United States of America

V 10 9 8 7 6 5 4 3 2 1

In memory of my mother
E. S.

To my mother and father
J. M.

Contents

Foreword: A Medical Opinion

The entourage of Nicholas II, czar of Russia, included an elite honor guard whose excessive drinking and eating of rich meats and mounds of caviar was legendary. Much to the chagrin of Nicholas II, the men of the honor guard had short life spans while the poor peasants, with their diet of grain and vegetables, lived longer.

An astute court doctor concluded that the rich diet caused the guardsmen's early deaths. And in 1908, A. I. Ignatowski, of Saint Petersburg, decided to test the theory. He fed rabbits with the honor guards' diet and the rabbits developed the honor guards' illness — arteriosclerosis. In years to follow, scientists were able to create arteriosclerotic plaques in similar experiments with dogs, chickens, and monkeys.

Epidemiological studies during the past 70 years have repeatedly demonstrated the role of cholesterol ingestion as an important factor causing hardening of the arteries. At the time of the Second World War, for example, none of the concentration camp victims, who were deprived of fats, showed any evidence of arteriosclerosis of the coronary arteries.

Young American soldiers killed during the Korean and Vietnam wars displayed advanced arteriosclerotic plaques in their arteries, while their Asian counterparts, who ate little fat, had none. A few years ago, the American Heart Association finally took a firm stand, advising a "prudent diet" for the American people: a diet low in cholesterol.

Weight reduction is fashionable and does have a great deal of medical merit, providing the diet followed doesn't endanger the well-being of the individual. For example, a diet rich in fat may slim you down but is likely to increase the deposit of fat in your arteries. To be convinced, one has only to witness an autopsy of a 60-year-old man and see the spoons of fat clinging to the walls of his arteries, impeding the flow of blood to vital organs like the heart. The main ingredient of these thickened deposits of fat is cholesterol — the cholesterol we obtain from eating such foods as milk, cheeses, eggs, butter, oils, and meats.

Arteriosclerosis is a disease that begins in childhood and ends with death. The appeal of a low-fat diet increases as new scientific evidence shows that arteriosclerosis may be a reversible disease. Animal experiments have demonstrated that arteriosclerotic infiltration of arteries can disappear if fat is entirely eliminated from the diet. And there are some reports demonstrating regression of arteriosclerosis in humans. X rays of diseased arteries were repeated after strict low-fat diet and showed dramatic improvement or disappearance of arterial narrowing presumed secondary to arteriosclerosis. Some patients suffering from angina (chest pain arising from diseased coronary arteries) find, when they are placed on the Pritikin diet, that their symptoms diminish and sometimes even disappear.

In the past few years, there have been fewer deaths from coronary artery disease, due, to a large extent, to the improvement in our diets. As a practicing cardiologist, I urge my patients to follow a strict low-fat diet with a generous increase of vegetables and complex carbohydrates (rice, beans, etc.) and with the elimination of meat and dairy products. The patient often laments, "What is there then left to eat?" *The Good Heart Diet Cookbook* shows that there is plenty. Finally, here is a sensible diet book written for the person who wants to follow a strict low-fat diet and still enjoy the pleasures of eating.

What a useful book to prescribe to my patients!

Siegfried J. Kra, M.D.
Associate Clinical Professor
Yale School of Medicine

Introduction

It was shocking to be told by my doctor that my cholesterol level was 385. Shocking because the "norm" is considered by the medical establishment to be between 150 and 250 — and mine was well above that. And shocking because I was only 25.

That was thirteen years ago. The cholesterol and I have been up and down since then. I was, for five years, a voluntary guinea pig in a research program, during which I imbibed large doses of two medicines: Colestid (before FDA approval) and Atromid-S (before it was suspected of causing cancer). I spent days of my life taking glucose tolerance tests. I swallowed two tablespoonsful a day of safflower oil — straight. I ate kegs of lecithin. I took aerobic dancing lessons. I took strange vitamins. I took tennis lessons. I jumped rope. I even tried acupuncture. I was willing to do anything but give up the food I loved.

When I found a cardiologist who told me I had a congenital problem, I was actually relieved. Aha! I thought, there's nothing I can do about it. And so I accepted his verdict that since my mother had died of atherosclerosis at the age of 51, and since her father had died of coronary heart disease at the age of 54, and since most of her aunts and uncles had also died of heart disease, I might too.

Of the 41,290,000 Americans with cardiovascular disease, 1,780,000 have had strokes; 4,400,000 have coronary heart disease; 35,520,000 have hypertension. Alarmingly, 1,500,000 may have a heart attack this year; 550,000 of them will die.

The legendary causes of heart attacks used to be smoking, drinking, obesity, lack of exercise, and stress. A best-selling theory in the seventies proposed the "Type A" personality — short-tempered, competitive, pressured — as the ideal heart-attack victim.

But it is now pretty much agreed among doctors and nutritionists that while these are indeed factors, more lethal by far is the diet high in cholesterol — specifically the high-fat hotdog-and-hamburger-and-pizza-and-ice-cream-cone American diet. Some cholesterol is necessary; our bodies even manufacture it for us. Too much is a very bad thing. It can clog the arteries, preventing blood from coursing through. Atherosclerosis — or "hardening of the arteries" — occurs in the large vessels such as the aorta and the coronary, and in the carotid, femoral, iliac, and cerebral arteries. Heart attacks happen. So do strokes.

Cholesterol itself is not a fat. It is a waxy solid. Masses of it form, adhere to the inside walls of the artery, and create an obstruction. The denser the masses, the smaller the boulevard. Brendan Phibbs, in his book *The Human Heart*, compares early atherosclerosis to "putty in a garden hose." Later on, the atheroma (fatty mass) can become "a hard, rocklike, chalky plaque, like a piece of cement on the lining of the artery. Early or late, fatty or chalky, an atheroma may grow to such a size that it blocks the ... artery completely, like a boulder damming a stream."

Pretty terrifying stuff.

For years, I continued flirting with guilt and danger. I was eating steaks and taking my medicine, eating lobsters and taking my medicine, eating chocolate cake and taking my medicine. My cholesterol level remained around 300. No one was pleased.

And then one July afternoon in 1978, during a routine eye examination, the doctor took a look through his ophthalmoscope. "Everything looks normal to me," he said. "And I can see some hardening of the arteries back there." I gasped, feeling that hot flush of panic, and then pale weakness. "That's *normal?*" I asked. "Sure," he said. "Especially in your case, where you have high cholesterol." Maybe he explained the situation to make me feel better. Maybe he didn't. I don't remember. All I could believe was that I was going to die. Soon.

The first thing I did was to stop eating altogether. The second thing I did was to find out about Nathan Pritikin, his Longevity Centers, his fast-walking regime, and his difficult diet. I liked what I learned — that the program would probably work for me. And so I registered for the next session at his center in Miami Beach.

At that time, Nathan Pritikin's name was just beginning to be heard in the land. There had been a few magazine articles about him, and a rather impressive segment on "60 Minutes," and patients were beginning to listen, but doctors were not. They argued that his diet was too severe, that most people would not stick to it, that his program didn't prove anything anyway since the long-range results weren't in. But Pritikin argued back that animals in meadows and tribes in jungles do not die of heart disease the way we do. And there's no reason that we need to either.

He believes that a cholesterol level over 165 is sufficiently dangerous to promote atherosclerosis (and this when most doctors accept levels up to 350). He advocates a high-fiber, high-carbohydrate diet, eliminating all animal fats, oil, nuts, egg yolks, sugar, alcohol, and caffeine. He allows neither saturated nor polyunsaturated fats, despite the fact that the American Heart Association recommends the latter. "In several respects," Pritikin writes in his excellent book, *The Pritikin Program for Diet and Exercise*, "unsaturated fats may be worse for you than saturated fats.... Both kinds of fats raise the triglyceride levels in the blood.... Polyunsaturates also deplete the body's vitamin E, are implicated in gallstone formation, and may well stimulate tumor growth."

It's very confusing. One day *The New York Times* publishes news of a report from the Food and Nutrition Board of the National Research Council: A reduced-cholesterol diet is not necessary for everybody, the dangers do not apply to us all. Four days later, the paper reports righteous indignation by government experts from the National Heart, Lung, and Blood Institute, the Department of Health and Human Services, the Department of Agriculture who suggest that the report was composed by consultants to the egg and dairy industries.

Different studies say that breast-fed babies may avoid atherosclerosis later on ... that vasectomies may bring it about ... that oral contraceptives raise cholesterol ... that vitamin C lowers it ... that shellfish are high in cholesterol ... that shellfish are low in cholesterol ... that sunflower oil is better than safflower oil is better than corn oil.

The New England Journal of Medicine reports that black tree fungus, a common ingredient in Chinese cooking, will prevent heart attacks because it slows blood-clotting. A patent is awarded Dr. Samuel Klein of New Jersey for a chicken-feed supplement to produce low-cholesterol eggs. And so it goes.

In August of 1978, I took leave of my office and flew to the Longevity Center in Florida. Twenty-six days later, suntanned and hard-legged, with my cholesterol plunging and ten pounds already lost, I returned to New York. Before I'd even unpacked my sand-filled suitcase, before I'd gone through the mail, before I'd even changed my sandals, I pulled out the shopping cart and headed for the health-food store and supermarket. Speed was essential, because I was scared. It was one thing to be among Pritikinized peers in Florida (at "heart camp," as my husband called it), and quite another to be alone with the crusade at home. I was now about to empty the larder — to throw out the peanut butter, cookies, jams, honeys, coffees, teas, olive oil, sugar, saccharin, anchovies, and cashews — and that was a serious commitment. (Ever dramatic, I entirely disregarded my husband's lusts — for peanut butter, cookies, jams, honeys, etc. — and hoped he would go on the wagon with me. He wouldn't. He went out directly and bought new jars of peanut butter, cookies, jams, honeys, etc.)

I came home from my shopping expedition with things I never would have considered eating before: healthy, high-fiber, high-carbohydrate things like navy beans, kidney beans, black beans, and lima beans. Lentils, barley, and brown rice. Chickpeas, split peas, and black-eyed peas. No cornflakes or Cheerios (made with sugar, salt, malt, etc.), but bags of cracked wheat for home-made cereal. No commercial breads (baked with oil, shortening, honey, molasses, sugar, salt, etc.), but a delicious discovery: Baldwin Hill sourdough bread made with stone-ground whole wheat (and available only in health-food stores). No avocados or olives (too oily), but bushels of grapefruits, oranges, lemons, apples, peaches, corn, potatoes, tomatoes, onions, eggplant, parsley, squash, celery, carrots, leeks, and — most important — garlic. Everything would be all right if I had enough garlic. Or so I thought.

Cooking classes at the Pritikin Center had been so inspiring that I'd assumed I would blithely prepare proper meals for the next ten years without worry. I was wrong. After a couple of weeks back in New York, the verve was gone. Everything tasted the same. Steamed vegetables tasted like sautéed vegetables — because both were done with water or with a vegetable stock (that was always too weak). Potatoes sliced and placed in the oven on a cookie tin simply did not taste like French fries. Ground chickpeas mixed with lemon, apple juice concentrate, and garlic did not remotely resemble hummus. And the beans had to be soaked overnight. And the vegetables took hours to mince and julienne. And seasoning things with soy sauce instead of salt made everything taste of soy sauce. I had been perfectly willing to put in the time if the results paid off. But they didn't, so I couldn't. I became despondent and stopped trying to be creative.

I stopped pretending to like carrot rings, zucchini casseroles, and turnip soup. I decided to simplify. I would major in austerity. Dinners became wan transactions of plain baked potatoes, plain steamed rice, plain steamed artichokes, dry tomato-and-onion salads. And my sympathetic husband, whose cholesterol is 142, would be kind. He would eat the vegetables with me — and also eat a hamburger, or a piece of chicken, or a lamb chop. And wine. And blueberry pie. And I would hate him. But we managed.

When we'd go out to dinner, we also managed. In Chinese restaurants, there were always steamed vegetables and rice. In Italian restaurants, there was always pasta and, if the waiter and chef were particularly solicitous, they would serve it with tomato sauce made on the spot, especially for me (which in most cases merely means opening a can of tomatoes and adding some onions and herbs). If the waiter and chef couldn't be bothered, however, there was always linguine with fresh lemon and freshly ground pepper. French restaurants were out, pretty much, as were Indian and Armenian and Greek and Spanish (*what?* cook without *oil?*). American restaurants always had a baked potato, or some lettuce. I did it. I still do.

But home is where the heart is. And home is where the heart is going to get healthier, since that's where most of the food gets eaten. So enter Jonathan Michaels.

As a senior editor at *New York* magazine, I was attending editorial lunches every week and bringing in my own tomato-and-mustard-on-pita-bread sandwiches until one lovely day, Jonathan, who was the magazine's executive chef, looked aghast and offered to prepare something special for me. I was happy to indulge him. And so week after week thereafter, while my colleagues dined on *poulet à la niçoise, bouillabaisse,* and cream puffs (and, on one peculiar occasion, on chicken-fried steak with cream gravy, mashed potatoes, and strawberry shortcake), I was crunching my way through craftily carved crudités, steamed cucumbers with lemon and fresh dill, leeks *à la provençale,* and banana whip. And I was newly inspired.

Suddenly, because of Jonathan Michaels, there were new

tastes, pretty plates, and, at home, a renaissance in the garden of my refrigerator! There was help beyond garlic, innovation beyond oregano! Jonathan feels that what you prepare can be one-step simple or quite complicated, but it should always be interesting. Use garlic, never garlic powder. Whenever possible, use fresh basil, parsley, dill, tarragon, and ginger — not dried. Use thyme, generously, and cinnamon, and curry powder, and mustard, and Tabasco. People with heart disease don't necessarily have stomach problems. Some of us victims are even gourmets.

Once upon a time — about 2500 B.C., as a matter of fact — man ate the way he should. According to Reay Tannahill, in her worthy work, *Food in History:* "The raw materials of the Sumerian diet were barley, wheat and millet; chickpeas, lentils and beans; turnips; onions, garlic, leeks; cucumbers; and fresh green lettuce, cress and mustard.... For 'civilized' man, grain had supplanted meat as the mainstay of the diet."

But today, because of the Good Life, even young children are found to be developing high cholesterol, and coronary artery disease is considered an epidemic. Cholesterol is in the news almost daily; the medical community is coming to agree with what Nathan Pritikin has said for years: The food we're living on can be killing us.

Pritikin maintains that atherosclerosis is reversible. So I am reversing mine. Having a husband and a baby boy I love gives me very good reason to want to live for a long time. And having Jonathan Michaels' recipes makes it possible. He has created dishes for people with a lifetime of too much fat in their diets and for people who simply want to lose weight. The recipes are, for those of us who insist on following a rigid regime, "legal." They are astoundingly inexpensive. And more than that, they are pleasing.

Ellen Stern
New York City

Cooking Techniques

Most of the techniques in this book are conventional. But, due to the special requirements of the diet, there are a few details that demand attention.

Fundamentally, food is cooked with either dry heat or wet heat. Dry heat is heat that is transferred from the source to the food through the medium of air, or metal, or any other means that does not require the food to be immersed in liquid; roasting, broiling, and sautéing are three of the most common dry-heat procedures. Moist-heat techniques use a liquid as the means of transferring heat. Boiling, poaching, braising, and stewing are all moist-heat methods.

We can use the moist-heat methods in the traditional way, but if we are to use the dry-heat techniques we must introduce some changes. Dry-heat cooking normally requires that the food be lubricated so it won't dry out or burn. Fats or oils are usually used, because they can sustain a high degree of temperature without burning or evaporating. (Oils have additional advantages as lubricants, but these are all beside the point since we can't use them.) We can and will use water, but, because water evaporates easily and tends to soak into food rather than remain on the surface, our dry-heat cooking will of necessity be limited.

When sautéing vegetables in water, it is generally best to heat the water in the pan before adding the food. In most cases, the food should be cut thin so that it will cook through quickly, leaving less time for it to become soggy. The ingredients should be stirred frequently so that they cook on all sides and don't stick to the pan. A medium flame should be used — hot enough to cook the food fairly quickly, but not so hot that the water evaporates too quickly. Onions can be put into cold water. This will help them become soft faster. Other vegetables can be sautéed as usual.

Boiling is one of the most common ways to cook vegetables, rice, and pasta. When boiling, use plenty of water — around two gallons for three pounds of food. This way, the water returns to a boil quickly after the food is added. (A warning: Don't cover green vegetables. They release a gas which, if contained, causes them to turn brown.) Make sure that the water is boiling hard before you add anything to it.

When boiling vegetables, the chief disadvantage is that vitamins tend to dissipate. Steaming leaves the vitamins where you want them: in the vegetables. It will be worth your while to buy a steamer. You can get a simple one that can be placed in the bottom of any pot, or a more elaborate utensil — a pot with up to three fitted baskets, one above the other — allowing you to steam three different items simultaneously.

Whether steaming or boiling, don't overcook your vegetables. Overdone vegetables lose vitamins, flavor, color, crispness; everything, in short, that makes vegetables worthwhile.

Many dishes, such as those containing vegetables and other legumes, are simmered rather than boiled. Simmering should be very gentle. The heat should be low enough so that the bubbles float to the surface without the explosive quality of boiling. This helps preserve both flavor and texture.

Another aspect of cooking that calls for special attention is the cutting of vegetables. It is a fact not generally appreciated that the way food is cut affects the way it tastes. Mushrooms sliced very thin will have a different effect in a dish than mushrooms sliced thick. In an oil-free, low-salt diet, the exploitation of a variety of textures becomes crucial to making food taste good. For this reason, you should learn to use knives well.

First, you should get some good ones. We'll go more into equipment in the next chapter, but for now, you should know that good, sharp knives will make your work easier and much more pleasurable. You should also have a large enough wood surface to work on; you shouldn't feel cramped for space. Your work surface should be low enough so that your body can be put into your work, but not so low that you can't stand upright. And you should have plenty of light to work by.

Hold your knife as though you were shaking someone's hand. As when learning any skill, you must have patience. Make haste slowly. If you try to mimic the Japanese chefs at Benihana, you'll probably only cut yourself.

If you develop a sense of rhythm in your use of a knife, you'll gain the speed you're after. Appreciate the possibilities of precision and smoothness. The more willing you are to be slow and exact in the beginning, the sooner you will find yourself becoming fast and exact. This applies to every aspect of cooking. Don't make a fetish of slowness, but do be constant in the matters of precision and rhythm.

8.

There are two fundamental knife techniques we should consider here, and they are slicing and chopping. Suppose you want to slice a carrot into rounds. The carrot is scraped and washed; you have cut both tips off. You stand facing the cutting squarely. You, the carrot, and your knife should form a triangle: the front of your body as the base, your left arm and the carrot as one side, your right arm and the knife as the other side. The apex of the triangle, where the knife meets the carrot, is also where you hold the carrot. The carrot rests on the table, and you hold it with your fingertips tucked in slightly; this avoids the inconvenience of cutting them off. The knife blade itself rests against the middle section of your fingers. It usually frightens people to have the blade so close to their hands but, in fact, this is your best insurance against accidents. As long as the blade slides flush against the middle section of your fingers, and your fingertips and thumb are tucked out of the way, you can't slip and cut yourself.

The tip of the blade should be touching the cutting board somewhere beyond the carrot. The blade itself is poised over the carrot. The actual cutting motion is a push from the upper part of your right arm. You push forward and down, then pull back and up, leaving the tip of the blade constantly in touch with the table. This gives you much more stability than lifting the blade from the table. Also, the diagonal motion of the knife lessens resistance and allows you to use more of your body weight. (Sometimes you'll have to slice something that is too high to leave the blade tip on the table. In that case, lift it as much as you have to, but leave the rest of the motion the same.)

Your left hand works intimately with your right. As the blade moves forward and down, backward and up, the left hand moves back along the carrot — faster for thick slices, slower for thin.

Chopping is, thank goodness, much easier to explain than slicing. Hold the knife in your right hand and place your left, fingers outstretched, on top of the end of the blade. The left hand gently holds the blade end down while the right hand moves up and down. The motion is essentially that of a paper cutter. Don't chop haphazardly, but move the blade steadily away from you, gather the chopped food together, and go through it again and again until it has reached the fineness you need.

We've looked at some techniques in this chapter that

should help you with the recipes in this book. There is, however, one final thing to take into account that may be more important than any other consideration: Use your own judgment. Many people take a mechanistic view of cooking, approaching recipes as though they were formulas for mixing cement. There are so many variables that no one can possibly achieve the best results this way. Some ovens get hotter than they should; some don't get hot enough. Sometimes you will be cooking young, tender green beans; sometimes older, tougher ones. You must develop an awareness of how these factors will affect your cooking and respond accordingly. If you acquire an appreciation of the qualities of the materials you are working with, equipment and food alike, you will find yourself almost unconsciously knowing what is the best way to handle them. Without this appreciation, cooking is joyless, tedious labor, and the results will reflect this attitude.

Stocking Your Kitchen

Below, you will find a list of pots and pans that you will need to prepare the dishes in this book. The only thing to keep in mind is that wherever possible, have nonstick utensils. Since we don't use butter or other oils, nonstick cookware is essential.

◆ Frying pans — three sizes should do it: 14-inch diameter for big dishes, 10-inch and 7-inch for others.

◆ Saucepans — 1½ quart, 4½-quart, 7-quart.

◆ Kettles — you should have a big one (16 quarts) for making stock and a smaller one (8 quarts) for sauces, etc.

◆ Nonstick jelly-roll pans — useful for vegetable casseroles. Two medium-sized ones (12 × 24 inches) should do it.

◆ Bread (loaf) pans — two 8-cup pans (9 × 5 × 2¾ inches).

◆ Knives — at the least, you need three of these: a 10- to 12-inch chef's knife, a small paring knife, and a serrated bread knife. High-carbon steel is good; high-carbon stainless steel is better. Plain stainless steel is not so good, as it does not hold a good edge.

◆ Miscellaneous utensils:
     Grater — the 4-sided kind
     Measuring cups — 4 cups, 2 cups, and 1 cup
     Dry-measure cups — 2 cups, 1 cup, ½ cup, ⅓ cup, ¼ cup
     Measuring spoons — 1 tablespoon, 1 teaspoon, ½ teaspoon,
         ¼ teaspoon, ⅛ teaspoon
     Food mill — for puréeing soups, etc.
     Lettuce dryer
     Two metal spoons — one with slots cut in it to let liquids
         through, the other unslotted
     Rubber spatula
     Wooden spoons and stirrers — only wood and rubber
         should be used on nonstick surfaces
     Long kitchen fork — to get into deep pots without burn-
         ing yourself
     Various wire whisks
     Pair of scissors
     Potholders
     Steaming basket — to steam vegetables
     Butcher-block chopping board — most people don't allow
         themselves enough room; try to get one at least
         2 × 2 feet
     Mortar and pestle
     Good pepper grinder
     Stainless-steel mixing bowls
     Colander
     Garlic press
     Blender
     Sharpening steel — for your knives

Stocking Your Larder

Herewith, a list of staples.

- Herbs and spices:
      dried basil
      bay leaves
      caraway seeds
      cayenne pepper
      chili pepper
      chili powder
      cinnamon, sticks and ground
      cloves, whole and ground
      cumin, ground
      curry powder
      fennel seeds
      ginger, fresh and powdered
      mace
      marjoram
      dried mint
      Dijon mustard
      nutmeg, whole and ground
      dried orange peel (which you can make yourself by peeling the rind off with a potato peeler and letting it dry)
      oregano
      peppercorns, black and white
      rosemary
      saffron
      sage
      savory
      tarragon
      thyme
      turmeric

♦ Dried legumes, grains, and pasta:
    black beans
    brown rice
    chickpeas
    Great Northern beans
    Jerusalem artichoke-flour pasta (recommended for its lighter hue and texture)
    kidney beans
    lentils
    lima beans
    pinto beans
    unbleached white flour
    whole-wheat flour

♦ Miscellaneous:
    apple juice concentrate (frozen)
    apple cider vinegar
    canned tomatoes (the imported Italian ones are best)
    cornstarch
    orange juice concentrate (frozen)
    soy sauce (or Tamari sauce)
    Tabasco
    tomato paste
    wine vinegar, red and white
    Worcestershire sauce

♦ A good suggestion:
    Grow an herb garden. The difference between fresh and dried basil, thyme, rosemary, etc. is astounding.

A Note on Adaptation

There are, in addition to the recipes in this book, recipes in hundreds of other cookbooks — simple ones, complicated ones, urban ones, provincial ones — that can be adapted to suit our austere needs.

Check the ingredients. Eliminate those (like egg yolks and bacon drippings) that are clearly taboo and impossible to fake. Learn the fine art of substitution: to think water instead of oil or melted butter, vegetable stock instead of beef broth, apple juice concentrate instead of sugar or honey, skim milk instead of heavy cream, a skim-milk and sage-flavored hard cheese called sapsago (an acquired taste, to be sure) instead of parmesan. And while dried fruits (raisins, apricots, currants, etc.) are too sugary for this diet, be consoled. A few drops of coconut, banana, or almond extract can do wonders.

This is a difficult diet — even more difficult than a vegetarian diet, which allows cheese, nuts, and honey — but it can become a pleasant part of life, especially when you see results. Welcome the challenge. Remember that necessity is, as it has always been, the mother of invention.

SOUPS

Potatoes have been a historical and international remedy for famine — just as they are here. The low-cholesterol diet is praiseworthy, to be sure, but it leaves you hungry! Thus, we offer a hearty selection of soups for lunch, for dinner, and any time in between. Many feature potatoes. Others feature pasta and beans. One cook we know thickens many of her soups by adding an extra puréed potato (instead of flour or cornstarch), which is a very good idea. And which leads to this note: Jonathan and Ellen disagree on the time indicated for soup-cooking. He likes his soups elegant, his vegetables recognizable. She prefers many of her soups thick, even if it means letting the vegetables become mushy. The longer the soup simmers, she figures (and this can mean days as well as hours), the heftier (and tastier) it gets.

Aïgo Bouido (Garlic Soup)

1 head garlic, cloves separated
½ teaspoon sage
½ bay leaf
1 teaspoon thyme
2 2-inch pieces of dried orange peel
2 cloves
Pinch of freshly ground black pepper
4 ounces whole-wheat or spinach spaghetti,
    broken (see pages 154–155)
¼ cup grated sapsago cheese
7 cups boiling water

*Bring a small pot of water to a boil, add the garlic,
and blanch it for 30 seconds.*
*Drain off the water, rinse the garlic under cold water, and
peel it.*
*Combine all the ingredients except the pasta and cheese
with 7 cups boiling water and boil slowly for 25 minutes.
Strain the soup into another pot, pressing the juices out
of the garlic. Bring soup to a boil, add the spaghetti, and
cook for 5 minutes.*
Sprinkle with sapsago cheese before eating.

SERVES 6

Asparagus Soup

2 large potatoes, peeled and cut into
   ¼-inch slices
2½ cups water
2 pounds asparagus, cooked until tender
1 teaspoon dried tarragon
½ cup white wine vinegar
½ teaspoon freshly ground black pepper
2 tablespoons cornstarch
6 cups Vegetable Stock (see page 47)
2 tablespoons fresh tarragon (if available)

Cook the potatoes in the water until tender, then purée.

Purée the asparagus, reserving tips. Add to potato purée and bring to a simmer.

Simmer tarragon, vinegar, and pepper together for 20 minutes.

Combine cornstarch with 8 tablespoons of the cold stock to make a smooth paste. Bring rest of the stock to a boil and stir in cornstarch. Cook for 5 minutes, then add asparagus-potato purée.

Add vinegar mixture. Stir to mix. Strain through a sieve. Bring to a boil.

Add fresh tarragon and asparagus tips and serve.

SERVES 6

Black Bean Soup

¾ pound dried black beans, soaked in cold water
   overnight
3 quarts cold water
Bouquet garni (1 bay leaf, 3 sprigs parsley,
   3 cloves)
¼ teaspoon freshly ground black pepper
2 onions, chopped
3 leeks, chopped
1 rib celery, chopped
2 carrots, chopped
Very thin lemon slices (for garnish)

*Drain beans and place in a stockpot. Add water
and bring to a boil.*

Reduce heat, skim, add bouquet garni and pepper.

*Cover and simmer until beans are tender (about 2½
hours).*

*Cook vegetables in 3 tablespoons water until onions are
translucent. Add to beans and simmer ½ hour more.*

*Skim surface, remove bouquet garni, and purée soup in a
food mill.*

Serve with lemon slices.

SERVES 6

Borscht

2 bunches beets, stems and leaves removed
2 quarts water
2 leeks, diced
1 medium boiled potato, mashed
½ teaspoon freshly ground black pepper
Fresh dill, chopped (for garnish)

*In 2 quarts of water, simmer beets until tender
(about 1 hour). Cook leeks in 3 tablespoons water until
soft. Add mashed potato and pepper and stir well.*
*Drain beets; add their water to leeks-potato-and-pepper
mixture.*
Peel and grate beets, add to soup, and chill.
Garnish with plenty of fresh, chopped dill.

SERVES 6

Broccoli and Pasta Soup

½ medium onion, very finely chopped
1 clove garlic, minced
1 tablespoon tomato paste
1 tablespoon soy sauce
4 cups water
¼ teaspoon freshly ground black pepper
Flowerets from 2 broccoli stalks
2 cups whole-wheat or spinach elbow macaroni
    (see pages 154–155)

Cook the onion with ¼ cup water in a pot. When the onion is soft, add the garlic and continue cooking for 2 minutes.

Add the tomato paste and soy sauce, stir well, then add 4 cups of water.

Bring the water to a boil and add the pepper and broccoli. Cook, uncovered, for 5 minutes.

Add the macaroni and cook for 10 minutes more.

SERVES 6

Cabbage Soup

    1 cup dried navy beans
    4 cloves garlic, mashed
    2 medium onions, thinly sliced
    ⅛ teaspoon ground chili pepper
    1 bay leaf
    ½ teaspoon marjoram
    ½ teaspoon thyme
    1 white cabbage, shredded
    3 turnips, peeled, quartered, and sliced
    ½ teaspoon freshly ground black pepper
    3 quarts water
    4 tablespoons red wine vinegar

Place the beans in a pot with water to cover and and bring to a boil. Continue cooking them for 2 minutes, then cover and let them stand for 1 hour.
Simmer the beans until tender, then drain them.
Combine all ingredients except vinegar, bring to a boil, and then simmer, covered, for 2 hours.
Remove bay leaf. Add vinegar, stir, and serve.

SERVES 6

Carrot Soup

1 onion, sliced thin
1 bay leaf
1 ½ pounds carrots, sliced
1 large potato, peeled and sliced thin
1 rib celery, sliced
⅛ teaspoon cayenne pepper
4 cups Vegetable Stock (see page 47)
Minced parsley (for garnish)

Cook the onion in ¼ cup water until soft. Add the bay leaf, carrots, potato, celery, cayenne, and stock and simmer until potato slices are tender.
Remove the bay leaf and purée the soup.
Garnish with parsley.

SERVES 6

Chestnut Soup

1 ½ pounds chestnuts, peeled and skinned
1 ½ quarts Vegetable Stock (see page 47)
1 cup hot skim milk

Simmer chestnuts in 3 cups of stock until tender. Purée and add the rest of the stock and the milk.

SERVES 6

Cauliflower Soup

¼ cup unbleached flour
4 cups water
1 medium head cauliflower
2 large leeks (white part only), well washed
    and sliced
2 medium onions, sliced
3 cups Vegetable Stock (see page 47)
½ teaspoon freshly ground black pepper
1 cup skim milk

Mix the flour with 1 cup of water, stirring until smooth.

Add the cauliflower, leeks, onions, stock, pepper, and 3 cups water.

Simmer for 1 hour, strain through a food mill, and add the skim milk. Heat gently and serve.

SERVES 6

Cherry Soup

1 ½ pounds sweet fresh cherries
6 cups water
¼ cup lemon juice
6 thin orange slices
¼ cup orange juice concentrate
1 ½ tablespoons cornstarch

Remove the pits from the cherries and set them aside.

Bring 5 cups of water to a boil. Add the cherries, lemon juice, orange slices, and apple juice concentrate, cover and simmer for 20 minutes.

Combine the cherry pits with 1 cup of cold water and cook over medium heat for 15 minutes.

Blend the cornstarch with a little cold water and add it to the cherry mixture. Strain in the liquid from the cherry pits. Cook the soup, stirring, until it becomes clear (about 1 minute).

Serve hot or cold.

SERVES 6

Chickpea Soup

1 cup dried chickpeas
1 medium onion, chopped
1 leek, chopped
½ cup canned tomatoes, chopped
1 clove garlic, minced
½ teaspoon rosemary
¼ teaspoon freshly ground black pepper
6 cups water
Juice of ½ lemon

Place the chickpeas in a pot with water to cover and bring to a boil. Continue cooking them for 2 minutes, then cover and let them stand for 1 hour.
Simmer until tender, then drain them.
Cook the onion, leek, tomatoes, garlic, and rosemary in ¼ cup of water until the onion is soft.
Add the cooked chickpeas, pepper, and 6 cups of water and simmer for 1 hour more.
Purée the soup in a food mill, then add the lemon juice and serve.

SERVES 6

Gazpacho

2 slices Whole-Wheat Bread (see page 151)
¼ cup vinegar
2 cloves garlic
2½ pounds canned tomatoes
1 medium onion, sliced
1 cucumber, peeled, seeded, and sliced
1 green pepper, quartered and seeded
1 cup Tomato Juice (see page 222)
2 cups Vegetable Stock (see page 47)
⅛ teaspoon cayenne pepper
½ cucumber, seeded and diced (for garnish)
½ green pepper, seeded and diced (for garnish)
¼ cup chopped parsley (for garnish)

Soak the bread in the vinegar.
Combine all the ingredients in a blender or food processor and purée them.
Transfer the soup to a bowl and chill in the refrigerator.
Garnish with diced cucumber, green pepper, and parsley.

SERVES 6

Spicy Gazpacho

3 ripe tomatoes
1 cucumber, peeled and cut into pieces
1 onion, peeled and quartered
1 clove garlic
1 teaspoon Worcestershire sauce
1 tablespoon crushed red pepper
½ cup diced green pepper (for garnish)
½ cup diced cucumber (for garnish)

Combine the tomatoes, cucumber, onion, garlic, Worcestershire sauce, and red pepper in a blender and purée until smooth.
Chill in the refrigerator, then serve with the diced pepper and cucumber.

SERVES 6

Leek and Potato Soup

4 leeks (white part only) cut into ⅓-inch dice
1 medium onion, cut into ⅓-inch dice
4 potatoes, cut into ½-inch dice
4 cups water
1 cup skim milk
¼ teaspoon freshly ground white pepper
1 tablespoon soy sauce

Cook the leeks and onion in ¼ cup of water until soft.
Add the potatoes and 4 cups of water, and simmer covered for 30 to 40 minutes.
Add the milk, pepper, and soy sauce. Stir and serve.

SERVES 6

Lentil Soup

    1 medium onion, chopped
    1 ½ cups lentils, washed and drained
    1 ripe tomato (or ⅓ cup canned tomatoes)
    2 carrots, chopped
    2 cloves garlic, peeled and crushed
    1 teaspoon thyme
    2 bay leaves
    4 cups water

In ¼ cup water, sauté the onion until translucent. Add everything and simmer until the lentils are soft (1 to 2 hours).
Remove bay leaves and purée ⅓ of the soup. Mix the purée back in and serve.

SERVES 6

Cold Melon Soup

    2 ripe cantaloupe melons (or any sweet melon)

Cut melons in half, remove seeds, and purée flesh in a blender.
Strain, chill, and serve.

SERVES 6

Minestrone

½ pound dried Great Northern beans
2 cloves garlic, minced
2 medium onions, thinly sliced
1 teaspoon rosemary
1 teaspoon chopped parsley
1 tablespoon tomato paste
2 carrots, peeled and diced
1 large rib celery, diced
1 zucchini, diced
1 cup shredded cabbage
½ cup canned tomatoes, chopped
1 clove
½ teaspoon freshly ground black pepper
10 cups cold water
1 cup whole-wheat elbow macaroni (see page 155)

Place the beans in water to cover and bring to a boil.
Cook 2 minutes, then let stand for 1 hour.
Combine garlic, onions, rosemary, and parsley with ¼ cup water and cook until the onions are soft.
Add the tomato paste and stir well. Add the carrots, celery, zucchini, cabbage, tomatoes, beans, clove, and pepper, plus 10 cups of water, and simmer 1 hour.
Add macaroni and cook 10 minutes more.

SERVES 6

Mushroom Soup

 1 pound mushrooms
 ¼ teaspoon freshly ground black pepper
 2 teaspoons lemon juice
 1 bunch watercress
 ¼ cup chopped shallots
 3 cups Vegetable Stock (see page 47)
 2 tablespoons cornstarch

Clean the mushrooms, then cut off and chop the stems. Slice the caps thin.
Combine the mushrooms with pepper, lemon juice, and 1 tablespoon water in a saucepan. Cover and cook for 10 minutes, stirring occasionally. Drain, reserving the liquid.
Chop the watercress and combine it in a saucepan with the shallots and mushroom liquid. Add 2¾ cups of the vegetable stock and all but 1 cup of the mushrooms and bring to a simmer.
Combine the cornstarch with ¼ cup cold stock and mix well.
Add it to the soup and simmer for 10 minutes.
In an electric mixer, blend the soup. Add the reserved mushrooms, reheat, and serve.

SERVES 6

Cream of Mushroom Soup

3 shallots, minced
1 clove garlic, minced
1 pound fresh mushrooms, chopped
4 tablespoons chopped parsley
½ bay leaf
Pinch of thyme
1 slice Whole-Wheat Bread (see page 151)
Skim milk
6 cups Vegetable Stock (see page 47)
2 teaspoons lemon juice

Cook the shallots and garlic in 3 tablespoons water until the shallots are soft.
Add the mushrooms, parsley, bay leaf, and thyme and cook them for 5 minutes over medium heat.
Soak the bread in a little skim milk and stir it in with the mushroom mixture.
Add the stock and simmer the soup for 15 minutes, remove bay leaf, then purée.
Stir in the lemon juice and serve.

SERVES 6

Onion Soup Gratiné

6 large onions, thinly sliced
7 cups cold water
Freshly ground black pepper to taste
6 slices Whole-Wheat Bread, toasted (see page 151)
¼ cup grated sapsago cheese

*Cook the onions in ½ cup water until very soft.
Add 7 cups cold water and pepper to taste, bring slowly
to a boil and simmer partially covered for 40 minutes.
Line the bottom of an ovenproof casserole with toast slices,
sprinkle with cheese, and pour hot soup over.
Place in a 400° oven until top bubbles.*

SERVES 6

Soupe au Pistou

¾ cup dried kidney beans
2 quarts water
2 cups diced onions
3 large boiling potatoes, peeled and diced
4 tomatoes, peeled, seeded, and chopped
¾ pound green beans, trimmed and cut into
    1-inch pieces
4 small zucchini, cut into large dice
1 cup whole-wheat or spinach spaghetti, broken up
    (see pages 154–155)
¼ teaspoon freshly ground black pepper
Pinch of saffron
½ cup fresh basil leaves, firmly packed
4 cloves garlic
¼ cup grated sapsago cheese

Place the beans in a pot with water to cover and bring to a boil. Continue cooking them for 2 minutes, then cover and let stand for 1 hour. Simmer the beans until tender, then drain them.

Bring 2 quarts of water to a boil. Add the onions and potatoes and simmer for 40 minutes.

Add the tomatoes, cooked kidney beans, green beans, zucchini, spaghetti, pepper, and saffron and cook for 15 minutes.

Just before serving, pound the basil, garlic, and cheese in a mortar until it forms a smooth paste. Stir it into the soup and serve.

SERVES 6

Potage Printanier

3 leeks, cut into small dice
1 small onion, cut into small dice
2 potatoes, thinly sliced
1 ½ cups hot water
5 cups Vegetable Stock (see page 47)
1 ½ pounds spinach leaves, finely shredded
1 cup watercress leaves, finely shredded
1 cup shelled peas
10 stalks asparagus, peeled and cut into
   ¼-inch rounds
¼ teaspoon freshly ground white pepper
Chopped parsley (for garnish)

Combine the leeks and onion in a stock pot with ¼ cup water, cover and cook them, stirring occasionally, until they are soft.
Add the potatoes and hot water, cover and simmer for 15 minutes.
Add the stock and bring it to a boil.
Add the spinach and watercress and simmer for 5 minutes.
Purée the soup.
Return soup to pot, bring to a boil, add the peas and asparagus, and simmer for 20 minutes.
Add the pepper.
Serve with plenty of chopped parsley.

SERVES 6

Pumpkin Soup

¾ cup chopped scallions
1 onion, minced
1 ½ cups Vegetable Stock (see page 47)
4 cups seeded, roughly chopped fresh pumpkin
1 bay leaf
¼ teaspoon freshly ground white pepper
1 small hot pepper, seeded and minced
½ cup skim milk, scalded

Cook the scallions and onion in the stock until soft.
Add the pumpkin, bay leaf, white pepper, and hot pepper, cover, and simmer 30 minutes.
Remove bay leaf and purée the soup, then add the skim milk to it.

SERVES 6

Spinach Soup

2 scallions, minced
1 small clove garlic, minced
4 well-packed cups spinach leaves, finely chopped
5 ½ cups Vegetable Stock, boiling (see page 47)
1 bay leaf
¼ teaspoon freshly ground black pepper
1 ½ tablespoons cornstarch mixed with a
    little water
1 tablespoon lemon juice

*Cook the scallions and garlic in ¼ cup water until
the scallions are soft.
Stir in the spinach, cover, and cook gently for 5 minutes.
Add the stock, bay leaf, pepper, and cornstarch; mix well
and simmer, stirring, for 5 minutes. Remove bay leaf.
Purée the soup, stir in the lemon juice, and serve.*

SERVES 6

Spinach and Potato Soup

4½ pounds fresh spinach
2 medium onions, chopped
9 new potatoes, peeled and sliced
3 cloves garlic
2 branches fennel
¼ teaspoon freshly ground black pepper
1 tablespoon soy sauce
1 quart water

Wash the spinach, then place the still-damp leaves in a large pot and cook, stirring occasionally, for 4 to 5 minutes. Remove the spinach from the pot and chop it.
In the same pot, cook the onions with ¼ cup water until they are soft.
Add all the other ingredients and cook until the potatoes are tender.

SERVES 6

Spinach-Yogurt Soup

5 shallots, finely chopped
1 pound fresh spinach, cut into large pieces
¾ cup brown rice, washed
¼ teaspoon freshly ground black pepper
5 cups water
2 cups Low-Fat Yogurt (see page 207)
2 cloves garlic, crushed

Cook the shallots with ¼ cup water until they are soft. Add the spinach and cook for 4 minutes.
Add the rice, pepper, and 5 cups of water and cook until the rice is just done.
Mix the yogurt with the garlic and add it to the soup, stirring well. Serve.

SERVES 6

Split Pea Soup

1 pound split peas
2 quarts water
2 medium onions, chopped
2 carrots, chopped
1 rib celery, chopped
¼ teaspoon powdered savory
Bouquet garni (1 bay leaf, 3 sprigs parsley,
    3 cloves)
2 cloves garlic
¼ teaspoon freshly ground black pepper

Combine all ingredients and bring to a boil. Cover pot, reduce to a simmer, and cook for 2 hours, stirring occasionally.
Remove bouquet garni and purée.

SERVES 6

Curried Squash Soup

2 medium acorn squash
3 cups Vegetable Stock (see page 47)
¼ cup orange juice concentrate
1 medium onion, chopped
1 clove garlic, mashed
1½ cups sliced mushrooms
½ teaspoon ground cumin
½ teaspoon cinnamon
¾ teaspoon ground ginger
¼ teaspoon dry mustard
¼ teaspoon cayenne
1 tablespoon lemon juice
Low-Fat Yogurt (see page 207) for garnish

Preheat oven to 375° F.
Split the squash lengthwise and place them in a nonstick baking pan. Bake until they are soft (about 30 minutes). Scoop out the flesh and purée it with the vegetable stock and orange juice concentrate.
Cook the onion, garlic, mushrooms, and spices with ½ cup water for 15 minutes.
Stir in the squash purée and lemon juice and heat the soup. Spoon yogurt over the top to serve.

SERVES 6

Tomato and Rice Soup

¾ cup thinly sliced onions
1½ pounds canned tomatoes, chopped (reserve juice)
4 large cloves garlic, mashed
5 cups Vegetable Stock (see page 47)
¼ cup brown rice
Bouquet garni (7 sprigs parsley, ½ bay leaf, ½ teaspoon thyme, 5 fennel seeds, ¼ teaspoon basil)
¼ teaspoon freshly ground black pepper
Pinch of saffron
3 tablespoons red wine vinegar

Sauté onions in ¼ cup water until soft. Add tomatoes (without juice). Add garlic and cook 3 minutes. Add tomato juice and stock, bring to a boil, and add rice. Add bouquet garni, pepper, saffron, and vinegar. Simmer partly covered for 30 minutes. Remove bouquet garni before serving.

SERVES 6

Vegetable Soup I

1 leek, well washed and thinly sliced
1 medium onion, thinly sliced
2 medium carrots, thinly sliced
1 celery rib, thinly sliced
¼ cup fresh parsley
2 large potatoes, thinly sliced
2 quarts water
½ cup diced fresh tomatoes
¼ teaspoon freshly ground white pepper
2 tablespoons soy sauce

Combine the leek, onion, carrots, celery, and parsley with ½ cup of water and cook, stirring occasionally, for 5 minutes.
Add the potatoes and 2 quarts of water. Bring to a boil and simmer uncovered for 1 hour.
Add the tomatoes, pepper, and soy sauce. Serve.

SERVES 6

Vegetable Soup II

3 carrots, peeled and cut into ¼-inch dice
3 small white turnips, peeled and cut into
    ¼-inch dice
1 large potato, peeled and cut into ¼-inch dice
2 ribs celery, cut into ¼-inch dice
7 cups water
¼ teaspoon freshly ground black pepper
½ cup shelled peas
3 cloves garlic, peeled and crushed

Lightly brown carrots, turnips, potato, and celery in a nonstick pot. Add water and bring to a boil, then lower heat and simmer for 10 minutes.
Add pepper, peas, and garlic and cook 10 minutes more.

SERVES 6

Vegetable Stock

2 leeks, well washed and thinly sliced
2 medium onions, thinly sliced
2 medium carrots, thinly sliced
2 parsnips, thinly sliced
4 cloves garlic
3 ribs celery, thinly sliced
4 large potatoes, diced
2 white turnips, diced
½ cup fresh parsley
½ teaspoon thyme
½ teaspoon dried basil
½ teaspoon freshly ground black pepper
1 gallon water
¼ cup soy sauce

Combine all ingredients except the soy sauce in a large kettle with 1 gallon of cold water. Bring slowly to a boil, lower the heat to a simmer, and cook for 2 hours. Drain, add the soy sauce, and store for future use.

Note: *For small portions, needed for steaming vegetables, freeze the stock in individual ice-cube holders.*

YIELD: 5 quarts

Vichyssoise

3 leeks, cut into ⅓-inch dice
1 medium onion, cut into ⅓-inch dice
3 potatoes, cut into ½-inch dice
3 cups hot water
3 cups skim milk
½ teaspoon freshly ground white pepper
Chopped chives (for garnish)

Cook leeks, onion, and potatoes in hot water until potatoes are mushy (about 35 minutes).
Strain through a food mill. Add milk and pepper and chill. Garnish with chives.

SERVES 6

Watercress Soup

3 medium onions, sliced
5 potatoes, peeled and sliced
2 cloves garlic
2 cups water
4 bunches watercress, roughly chopped
2 cups skim milk mixed with 3 cups water
½ teaspoon freshly ground black pepper

Cook onions, potatoes, and garlic in 2 cups water until potatoes are quite soft. Add watercress, milk and water mixture, and pepper and bring to a boil. Strain through a food mill.

SERVES 6

White Bean Soup

2 ½ cups dried white beans
2 leeks, chopped
1 onion, chopped
1 rib celery, chopped
1 cup canned tomatoes
½ cup finely chopped parsley
¼ teaspoon freshly ground white pepper
½ teaspoon thyme
3 cups Vegetable Stock (see page 47)
4 cups water
2 cloves garlic
¾ cup fresh basil
¼ cup grated sapsago cheese

Place the beans in a pot with water to cover and bring to a boil. Continue cooking them for 2 minutes, then cover and let stand for 1 hour.
Simmer the beans until tender, then drain them.
Cook the leeks and onion with ¼ cup water until soft.
Add the celery, tomatoes, parsley, pepper, and thyme and cook gently for 5 minutes.
Add the cooked beans, stock, and water and simmer for 15 minutes.
Purée the soup.
Combine the garlic, basil, and cheese in a mortar and mash them to a paste. Beat paste into the soup.

SERVES 6

50.

Zucchini Soup

6 zucchini, cut into 1-inch cubes
Salt
2 onions, finely chopped
1 clove garlic, minced
2 cups Vegetable Stock (see page 47)
3 cups Low-Fat Yogurt (see page 207)
2 teaspoons lemon juice
1 tablespoon finely chopped parsley
2 tablespoons finely chopped fresh basil
2 teaspoons finely chopped chives
¼ teaspoon freshly ground black pepper

*Place the zucchini cubes in a colander, sprinkle
with salt, and toss lightly. Allow them to stand ½ hour
and then rinse thoroughly with cold water.*

*Cook the onions and garlic in ¼ cup water until the
onions are soft.*

*Add the zucchini and stock and cook over low heat for
15 minutes.*

Purée the soup and allow to cool.

Beat in the yogurt, lemon juice, herbs, and pepper.

Chill before serving.

SERVES 6

Elizabeth's Curried Zucchini Soup

1 medium onion, sliced
1 tablespoon powdered ginger
2 tablespoons curry powder
Pinch of saffron
½ hot chili pepper, seeded and finely chopped
2 large potatoes, peeled and sliced
7 cups water
1 ½ pounds zucchini, sliced
1 tablespoon fresh basil (or 1 teaspoon dried)
½ cup Low-Fat Yogurt (see page 207)

Cook the onion gently in a soup pot with ¼ cup water for 3 to 4 minutes. Add the ginger, curry powder, saffron, and chili pepper and cook 3 minutes more.
Add the potatoes and stir them well. Then add 7 cups of water, stir, cover, and simmer for 30 minutes.
Stir in the zucchini and basil, cover the pot, and cook for 20 minutes more.
Purée the soup and strain it.
Stir in the yogurt and serve.

SERVES 6

VEGETABLES

In whatever order they made their debut — scorned as weeds, admired as ornamentation, and, of course, eaten — vegetables remain versatile, colorful, ubiquitous, and made up mostly of water. What's more, vegetables are popular. They have their lore (many, from carrots to shallots to truffles to radishes, have been touted as aphrodisiacs), their lyrics, and their devotees. The Emperor Nero liked leeks, the Emperor Augustus went for asparagus, Aristotle admired cabbage. And, while Dracula was turned off by garlic, this fascinating herb has been used throughout history in the treatment of leprosy, fainting, whooping cough, cancer, the common cold, earache, ringworm, and even arteriosclerosis.

Steamed Artichokes with Lemon

6 artichokes
3 lemons
¼ cup parsley, finely chopped (for garnish)
Freshly ground black pepper

Trim tough bottom leaves off artichokes, cut off tips of other leaves with scissors, and remove stems.
Rub all exposed cut surfaces with a lemon cut in half (this prevents their turning brown).
Fill a large pot with water and the juice of ½ lemon to a depth of 1 inch and bring it to a boil.
Arrange artichokes in pot, stem side up; lay a wet towel over the top of the pot (this prevents too much steam from escaping) and place cover on top.
Cook over medium heat until artichokes are tender (about ¾ hour).
Serve with sliced lemon, chopped parsley, and fresh pepper.

SERVES 6

Asparagus with Tomato Sauce

 1 onion, finely chopped
 2 cloves garlic, minced
 6 canned tomatoes, chopped
 2 tablespoons tomato paste
 ½ teaspoon freshly ground black pepper
 1 teaspoon finely chopped parsley
 2 teaspoons finely chopped basil
 2 pounds asparagus

*Cook onion and garlic in ¼ cup water. Add toma-
toes, tomato paste, and pepper and cook, stirring, for 10
minutes. Stir in parsley and basil.*
*Cut off thick ends of asparagus. Peel stalks from below
tips to the ends. Cook 8 to 10 minutes in plenty of boiling
water.*
Drain and serve with sauce.

SERVES 6

Baba Ghanouj

1 large eggplant
¼ cup Hummus (see page 129)
2 small cloves garlic, mashed
3 tablespoons lemon juice
Pinch ground cumin

Preheat oven to 400°F.
In a nonstick baking dish, bake eggplant for 40 minutes.
When it has cooled somewhat, peel it and discard skin.
Place the flesh in a bowl and mash it with a fork.
Add the other ingredients and mix well.
Serve at room temperature with toasted whole-wheat pita bread.

SERVES 6

Beets with Ginger

3 ½ pounds beets
½ cup cider vinegar
1 tablespoon cornstarch dissolved in 2 tablespoons
   cold water
1 teaspoon finely chopped fresh ginger
¼ cup orange juice concentrate

Cut most of stem and roots off beets, leaving 1 inch on either end. Wash well. Fill pot with enough water to cover beets and bring to a boil.

Cook the beets until tender; this can take 1 to 2 hours, depending on their size. When they're done, drain and peel them; skins will slip off.

Combine all other ingredients in a saucepan and bring to a boil. Stir until clear. Lower heat and add beets, heating through gently.

SERVES 6

Broccoli Purée

4 heads broccoli, stem bottoms removed
¼ cup hot Vegetable Stock (see page 47)
2 small cloves garlic, mashed
½ teaspoon freshly ground black pepper
1 tablespoon lemon juice

Cook broccoli in plenty of boiling water until tender (about 15 minutes). Purée through a food mill. Beat in other ingredients.

SERVES 6

Broccoli Vinaigrette

½ cup white wine vinegar
6 scallions, minced
2 tablespoons parsley, minced
2 cloves garlic, crushed
2 teaspoons thyme
¼ teaspoon freshly ground black pepper
4 heads broccoli, stalks trimmed and peeled

Simmer everything except broccoli for 15 minutes. Meanwhile, blanch broccoli in plenty of boiling water for 10 minutes. Pour dressing over it. Serve chilled or at room temperature.

SERVES 6

Curried Brussels Sprouts

2 quarts Brussels sprouts
1 medium onion, finely chopped
2 teaspoons curry powder
1 tablespoon cornstarch mixed with ¼ cup
   cold water
2 cups hot Vegetable Stock (see page 47)
Bouquet garni (4 sprigs parsley, ½ teaspoon
   thyme, 1 bay leaf)
¼ teaspoon freshly ground black pepper

Trim the outside leaves of the sprouts.
Cook the onion gently with ¼ cup water until soft.
Add the curry powder and stir well.
Add the cornstarch mixture, stir and cook 1 minute.
*Pour the vegetable stock all at once into the pan and stir
with a wire whisk over medium heat.*
*When the liquid has thickened, add the bouquet garni,
pepper, and the Brussels sprouts; cover, and simmer gently
for 20 minutes.*

SERVES 6

Brussels Sprouts Purée

1 ½ pounds Brussels sprouts, trimmed
¼ teaspoon freshly ground nutmeg
1 tablespoon lemon juice
¼ cup skim milk

*Cook the sprouts in plenty of simmering water for
10 minutes.*
Purée the sprouts.
*In a saucepan, blend the purée with nutmeg, lemon juice,
and skim milk. Cook over low heat, stirring, for 5 minutes.*

SERVES 6

Cabbage Stuffed with Chestnuts and Mushrooms

1 large white cabbage
½ pound shelled chestnuts
¼ pound sliced mushrooms
¼ teaspoon freshly ground black pepper
¼ teaspoon thyme
⅛ teaspoon ground nutmeg
1 ½ cups Vegetable Stock (see page 47)
1 tablespoon soy sauce

Bring plenty of water to boil in a large pot and cook the cabbage for 10 minutes. Drain it and remove the outermost leaves.

Carefully spread the cabbage leaves outward, then cut out the hard inside core.

Mix the chestnuts, mushrooms, pepper, thyme, and nutmeg and stuff the cabbage with them. Reshape the leaves around the stuffing and fasten them into shape with a couple of pieces of masking tape.

Place the cabbage in a pot which will just hold it.

Pour on the stock and soy sauce, cover, and cook in a 350°F oven for 3 hours. Check occasionally to see if more stock is needed.

SERVES 6

Red Cabbage with Apples I

3 onions, chopped
¼ cup red wine vinegar
½ cup Vegetable Stock (see page 47)
1 2-pound red cabbage, shredded
¼ teaspoon caraway seed
2 greening or Granny Smith apples, peeled,
    cored, and diced
¼ teaspoon freshly ground black pepper

Cook the onions with the vinegar and stock until soft.
Add the other ingredients, stir, cover, and cook gently for 20 minutes.

SERVES 6

Red Cabbage with Apples II

1 head cabbage, shredded
3 greening apples, peeled, cored, and thinly sliced
⅛ teaspoon crushed clove
6 fennel seeds
¼ cup red cider vinegar
¼ cup apple juice concentrate

Combine all ingredients in a large skillet and cook over medium-low heat for 45 minutes.

SERVES 6

Red Cabbage and Chestnuts

2 pounds red cabbage leaves, cut into ½-inch slices
2 cups diced greening apples
2 cloves garlic, mashed
1 bay leaf
⅛ teaspoon ground clove
¼ teaspoon freshly ground black pepper
½ cup red wine vinegar
2½ cups Vegetable Stock (see page 47)
6 tablespoons apple cider vinegar
24 peeled chestnuts

Combine all ingredients except the chestnuts and cook in a 325°F oven for 3½ hours.
Add chestnuts and cook 1½ hours more. Discard bay leaf and serve.

SERVES 6

Stuffed Cabbage

1 2-pound head cabbage, trimmed
½ cup whole-wheat bread crumbs (see page 151)
¼ cup brown rice
½ teaspoon freshly ground black pepper
½ cup shelled peas
¼ cup chopped scallions (with greens)
Vegetable Stock to cover (see page 47)
1 clove garlic
3 sprigs parsley
Bouquet garni (1 bay leaf, pinch of thyme, a few
    fennel seeds)

*Simmer cabbage in water to cover for 10 minutes.
Without pulling off outer leaves, carefully pull out the
inner core, chop it fine, and mix with the bread crumbs,
rice, pepper, peas, and scallions.*
*Stuff the hollowed-out cabbage with this mixture and
wrap the entire assemblage in cheesecloth.*
Place in a heavy pot and cover with vegetable stock.
*Add garlic, parsley, and bouquet garni and simmer gently
for 2½ hours.*
Remove bouquet garni and serve.

SERVES 6

Marinated Baby Carrots

3 dozen baby carrots, peeled and trimmed
2 cloves garlic, sliced
½ teaspoon freshly ground black pepper
1 teaspoon oregano
1 cup Vegetable Stock (see page 47)
½ cup red wine vinegar

Combine all the ingredients in a pan and bring to a boil.
Simmer for 5 minutes, then let cool.
Chill overnight or longer before serving.

SERVES 6

Braised Carrots

12 carrots, peeled and thinly sliced
5 scallions, chopped
½ teaspoon finely chopped fresh ginger
1 tablespoon orange juice concentrate
¼ teaspoon freshly ground black pepper
1 cup Low-Fat Yogurt (see page 207)

Combine the carrots, scallions, ginger, and orange juice concentrate with 3 tablespoons water in a saucepan. Cover and cook gently for 15 minutes.
Stir in pepper and yogurt and heat through. Serve.

SERVES 6

Cauliflower with Fennel

2 heads cauliflower
⅓ cup red wine vinegar
1 tablespoon grated orange peel
¼ teaspoon freshly ground black pepper
1 stalk fennel, cut into ½-inch slices

Cook the cauliflower for 10 minutes in plenty of boiling water. Cut it into flowerets.
Combine the vinegar, orange peel, and pepper with the cauliflower and fennel in a skillet and cook, tossing, for 5 minutes.

SERVES 6

Celeriac Purée

3 baking potatoes, peeled
3 large celery roots, peeled
¼ cup Vegetable Stock (see page 47)
¼ teaspoon freshly grated nutmeg
½ teaspoon freshly ground black pepper

Place potatoes and celery roots in simmering water to cover and cook until just tender enough so that a fork pierces them easily.
Purée through a food mill or in a blender, then beat in other ingredients.

SERVES 6

Celery in Tomato Sauce

12 large ribs celery, leaves trimmed
½ medium onion, chopped
1 small clove garlic, minced
2 cups Vegetable Stock (see page 47)
¼ teaspoon freshly ground black pepper
1 cup Tomato Sauce (see pages 175–176)

Cut each rib of celery into thirds. Combine the celery, onion, garlic, stock, and pepper in a pan and simmer for 20 minutes, or until the celery is tender.
Serve with tomato sauce.

SERVES 6

Braised Chestnuts and Brussels Sprouts

¼ pound mushrooms, sliced
1 teaspoon tomato paste
2 cups Vegetable Stock (see page 47)
1 tablespoon cornstarch, dissolved in 2 tablespoons
   cold water
1 bay leaf
1 pound chestnuts, peeled
1 pound Brussels sprouts, outer leaves trimmed
1 tablespoon lemon juice
¼ teaspoon freshly ground black pepper

Preheat oven to 325°F.
Cook the mushrooms with 1 tablespoon water until they are soft. Stir in the tomato paste.
Stir the stock into the cornstarch mixture, then add it with the bay leaf to the mushrooms.
Add the chestnuts and place the dish in the oven for 45 minutes.
Place the sprouts in cold water and bring to a boil.
Drain them in a colander and place them in a skillet with the lemon juice and 3 tablespoons water. Cook them until just tender (about 8 minutes).
Add with pepper to the chestnuts, remove bay leaf, and serve.

SERVES 6

Poached Chestnuts

1 pound chestnuts, peeled
½ cup red wine
½ cup red wine vinegar
2 ribs celery
2 bay leaves

Combine all ingredients and simmer until tender (about 45 minutes). Remove bay leaves before serving.

SERVES 6

Chestnut Purée

1 pound chestnuts, peeled
3 ribs celery
1 onion
Bouquet garni (1 bay leaf, 4 sprigs parsley,
    ¼ teaspoon thyme)
Vegetable Stock to cover (see page 47)
¼ teaspoon freshly ground black pepper
¼ teaspoon nutmeg
2 tablespoons skim milk

Combine chestnuts, celery, onion, bouquet garni, and stock in a saucepan. Simmer until chestnuts are tender, but not mushy.
Remove chestnuts and purée in a food mill.
Add pepper, nutmeg, and skim milk.

SERVES 6

Roasted Chestnuts

1 ½ pounds chestnuts

Make a slit on the flat side of each nut. Place in a skillet and cook over high heat, shaking skillet, until nuts are almost black.
Peel and serve.

SERVES 6

Chestnut Soufflé

1 ½ pounds chestnuts, peeled
1 ½ cups Vegetable Stock (see page 47)
⅛ teaspoon ground nutmeg
⅛ teaspoon ground clove
¼ teaspoon freshly ground black pepper
2 egg whites

Preheat oven to 350°F.
Boil chestnuts in water to cover until just tender.
Purée in a food mill. Place in a pan with stock and spices and cook, stirring, until stock evaporates.
Beat whites until stiff and fold into chestnut mixture.
Pour into a nonstick baking dish and bake for 25 minutes.

SERVES 6

Cucumbers à la Grecque

1 large onion, minced
1 carrot, minced
3 large cucumbers, peeled and seeded
Bouquet garni (1 bay leaf, pinch of thyme,
    3 sprigs of parsley)
6 crushed peppercorns
8 coriander seeds
3 tablespoons white wine vinegar
Juice of 1 lemon
1 cup water

In a pot, cook the onion and carrot with ¼ cup water until the onion is soft.
Cut the cucumbers into large dice and add with the other ingredients to the onion and carrot.
Add 1 cup water and simmer for 5 minutes.
Remove the pot from the heat and allow it to cool.
Chill to serve.

SERVES 6

Pickled Cucumbers and Onions

12 small cucumbers
12 small white onions, peeled
2 cups white wine vinegar
1 small chili pepper, seeded and finely chopped
3 cloves garlic
2 bay leaves
1½ quarts water
¼ cup fresh dill leaves

Combine the cucumbers and onions in a jar.
Combine the vinegar, chili pepper, garlic, and bay leaves
with 1½ quarts water in a pot. Bring it to a boil and sim-
mer 5 minutes.
Turn off the heat and pour the mixture over the cucum-
bers and onions. Place the dill on top.
Cover the jar with cheesecloth and allow it to reach room
temperature. Refrigerate 1 week before serving.

SERVES 6

Steamed Cucumbers and Asparagus

3 cucumbers, peeled
6 stalks asparagus, peeled
3 tablespoons lemon juice
½ teaspoon freshly ground black pepper
2 tablespoons chopped fresh mint

Cut cucumbers in half lengthwise. Scoop out the seeds with a spoon, cut in half lengthwise again, and cut across in 1-inch pieces.
Cut asparagus in ¾-inch rounds. Mix the two vegetables and steam for 6 to 8 minutes or until just tender.
Stir with lemon juice, pepper, and mint, and serve.

SERVES 6

Cucumber Tea Sandwiches

1 large cucumber, peeled and sliced thin
¼ cup red wine vinegar
¼ teaspoon freshly ground black pepper
1 bunch watercress
6 thin slices of Whole-Wheat Bread, toasted and cut in triangles (see page 151)

Soak cucumber slices in vinegar for 5 minutes. Drain, add pepper, and place with a sprig of watercress between slices of toast.

SERVES 6

Duxelles

1 pound mushrooms, finely chopped
1 large onion, finely chopped
1 clove garlic, minced
1 tablespoon parsley, finely chopped (for garnish)

Sauté mushrooms gently in a nonstick skillet with 2 tablespoons water until they have rendered a few table-spoons of their juice. Remove mushrooms with a slotted spoon and add onion and garlic to skillet.
Cook until onion is translucent. Add mushrooms and cook 5 minutes, adding a little water if necessary.
Sprinkle with parsley and serve.

SERVES 6

Eggplant with Duxelles

2 medium eggplants, peeled
2 cups Duxelles (see page 74)
2 cups chopped parsley

Preheat oven to 400°F.

Cut the eggplants into ¼-inch slices. Set aside the end slices and use them for another purpose.

Place the outermost slice flat in a baking pan and spread it with duxelles. Place the next slice on top of it and spread it with duxelles. Go on repeating the layers until you have reconstructed both eggplants side by side in the baking dish minus the round outermost slices.

Bake the eggplants for 15 to 20 minutes, or unil tender. Remove them from the oven and set them on a warm serving platter. Coat the outside surface with chopped parsley.

SERVES 6

Grilled Eggplant

2 medium unpeeled eggplants
Freshly ground black pepper
1 lemon, cut in wedges

Place eggplants close to flame, rotating them so that the skin starts to char and peel all over. Cut them in wedges lengthwise, sprinkle with pepper, and serve with lemon wedges.

SERVES 6

Eggplant Purée

2 eggplants
¾ cup Low-Fat Yogurt (see page 207)
Juice of ½ lemon
2 cloves garlic, crushed
2 tablespoons finely chopped parsley

Place the eggplants under the broiler and cook them on all sides until the skin turns black and starts to blister. Rub the skin off, then gently squeeze out as much of the juice as possible.
Mash the eggplant to a paste.
Add the yogurt, lemon juice, garlic, and parsley and mix well.
Chill to serve.

SERVES 6

76.

Baked Endive

12 Belgian endives
¼ teaspoon freshly ground black pepper
½ cup Vegetable Stock (see page 47)
2 tablespoons finely chopped parsley
2 cloves garlic, minced
2 shallots, finely chopped
3 tablespoons lemon juice

Preheat oven to 350°F.
Place the endives in a baking dish and sprinkle with pepper.
Add the stock, cover the dish, and place it in the oven for
45 minutes.
Remove the endives from the dish and reserve them.
Add the parsley, garlic, shallots, and lemon juice to the
baking dish and stir over high heat for 45 seconds to 1
minute. Pour this mixture over the endives.

SERVES 6

Green Beans à la Chinoise

1 ½ pounds green beans
1 medium onion, sliced thin
½ teaspoon turmeric
3 cloves garlic, minced
1 teaspoon chopped fresh ginger
¼ cup canned tomatoes, chopped
2 dashes Tabasco
2 teaspoons lemon juice
1 tablespoon chopped cilantro (fresh coriander)

Cook the beans for 4 minutes in plenty of boiling water. Drain and run under cold water. Drain again and set aside.

Cook the onion in ¼ cup water until soft.

Add the turmeric and cook, stirring, for 2 to 3 minutes.

Add the garlic, ginger, tomatoes, Tabasco, and lemon juice and cook them gently for 10 minutes.

Add the beans and stir well. Cook everything together for 5 minutes, sprinkle with cilantro, and serve.

SERVES 6

Green Beans with Mustard

1 ½ pounds green beans, trimmed
½ cup Low-Fat Yogurt (see page 207)
¼ cup chopped cilantro (fresh coriander)
1 teaspoon Dijon mustard
1 tablespoon lemon juice

Cook the beans in plenty of boiling water for 6 minutes. Drain, rinse under cold water, and drain again. Mix the other ingredients and add them to the beans. Stir and chill to serve.

SERVES 6

Green Beans Provençale

1 ½ pounds green beans, trimmed
2 onions, thinly sliced
2 cloves garlic, minced
1 cup canned tomatoes
½ green pepper, chopped
¼ teaspoon freshly ground black pepper
1 bay leaf
2 teaspoons chopped parsley
1 strip dried orange peel

Bring plenty of water to boil in a pot with a steaming basket. Add the green beans, cover, and steam for 5 minutes. Remove the beans from the pot and rinse under cold water.

Heat ⅓ cup water in a skillet. Add the onions and cook them until they are soft. Add the garlic, tomatoes, green pepper, black pepper, bay leaf, parsley, and orange peel, plus ¼ cup water, and simmer, uncovered, for 20 minutes. Add the beans, stir, and cook them until they are heated through.

SERVES 6

Spicy Green Beans

1 pound fresh green beans, trimmed
2 tablespoons finely chopped fresh ginger
3 tablespoons chopped scallions
2 tablespoons soy sauce
2 leaves Chinese cabbage, blanched and chopped
¼ cup Vegetable Stock (see page 47)
2 tablespoons chopped cilantro (fresh coriander)

Cook the beans in plenty of boiling water for 4 minutes. Drain, run cold water over them, and drain again. Combine the ginger, scallions, soy sauce, cabbage, stock, and cilantro in a nonstick skillet and cook for 2 minutes. Add the beans, stir, and heat through. Serve.

SERVES 6

Jerusalem Artichokes à l'Italienne

1 ½ pounds Jerusalem artichokes, peeled
4 canned tomatoes, chopped
¼ teaspoon dried basil
1 clove garlic, minced
1 green pepper, seeded and cut into small dice
2 dashes Tabasco

Cook artichokes in simmering water to cover for 20 minutes. Drain well and combine in a skillet with other ingredients. Simmer 12 minutes, stirring occasionally.

SERVES 6

Leeks with Mustard Sauce

12 large leeks, cleaned
½ teaspoon freshly ground black pepper
1 teaspoon Dijon mustard
2 tablespoons red wine vinegar
Whites of 4 hard-cooked eggs
⅓ cup finely chopped parsley
Romaine lettuce leaves

Simmer leeks in a large pot of water for 8 minutes or until tender. Drain and rinse under cold water. Drain again.

Mix pepper, mustard, and vinegar. Chop egg whites fine. Add egg whites and parsley to vinegar mixture and stir well.

Place leeks on leaves of Romaine lettuce and spoon dressing over them.

SERVES 6

Leeks Provençale

½ cup canned tomatoes with their juice
2 bay leaves
3 cloves garlic
12 leeks, trimmed and washed well
3 tablespoons finely chopped fresh basil
   (or 1 ½ teaspoons dried)
1 tablespoon oregano
3 tablespoons lemon juice
¼ teaspoon freshly ground black pepper

Combine the tomatoes, bay leaves, garlic, and leeks in a skillet. Cover and simmer gently for 15 minutes, stirring occasionally. Add the basil and oregano and cook 3 minutes more.
Remove from the heat and add the lemon juice and pepper. Remove the bay leaves.
Chill to serve.

SERVES 6

Maize alla Limeña

3 ½ cups fresh corn, cut and scraped from the cob
1 cup skim milk
½ cup coarsely chopped onion
½ cup coarsely chopped carrots
½ cup coarsely chopped celery
½ teaspoon thyme
1 tablespoon chopped fresh basil
2 teaspoons paprika
¼ teaspoon freshly ground black pepper
1 cup cooked lima beans

Place the corn and milk in a blender and blend to lightly mash the kernels.
Combine the onion, carrots, celery, thyme, basil, paprika, and pepper with ½ cup water and cook, stirring occasionally, for 10 minutes.
Add the lima beans and corn mixture and cook for 10 minutes more.

SERVES 6

Marinated Mushrooms

> 3 cloves garlic, mashed
> 3 tablespoons Dijon mustard
> ½ cup white wine vinegar
> 2 tablespoons lemon juice
> ¼ teaspoon freshly ground black pepper
> 1 tablespoon dried tarragon
> 1½ cups Vegetable Stock (see page 47)
> 1 pound small mushrooms, trimmed

Combine the garlic and mustard and beat well. Beat in the vinegar, lemon juice, pepper, tarragon, and vegetable stock.
Place the mushrooms in a large bowl, pour the marinade over them, and toss well. Cover and chill overnight.

SERVES 6

Mushrooms Marinara

> 1½ pounds mushrooms, sliced
> 2 cups Tomato Sauce II (see page 176)

Sauté mushrooms gently with ⅓ cup water until they soften.
Pour tomato sauce over them and serve.

SERVES 6

Stuffed Mushroom Caps

36 large mushrooms, wiped clean
3 tablespoons parsley, finely chopped
1 clove garlic, minced
6 tablespoons fine whole-wheat bread crumbs
(see page 151)
¼ teaspoon freshly ground black pepper

Pull the stems off the mushrooms. Trim the ends and chop the stems fine.
Cook the stems with 2 tablespoons water for 5 minutes.
Turn off the heat, add the parsley, garlic, bread crumbs, and pepper and mix well.
Stuff the mushroom caps with this mixture and arrange them, hollow side up, on a broiling pan.
Place them 4 to 6 inches away from the heat and broil them for 5 minutes.

SERVES 6

Okra with Tomatoes

1 ½ pounds okra, trimmed and sliced
3 onions, sliced thin
1 cup canned tomatoes, chopped
¼ teaspoon oregano
¼ teaspoon freshly ground black pepper

Cook the okra for 3 minutes in plenty of boiling water. Drain and run under cold water.
Cook the onions in ¼ cup water until soft.
Add the tomatoes, oregano, and pepper and cook gently for 15 minutes.
Add the okra, stir, and heat it through.

SERVES 6

Boiled White Onions

30 small white onions
¼ cup chopped mixed parsley and fresh basil
½ teaspoon freshly ground black pepper

Trim the ends of the onions and peel the outer skins. Bring plenty of water to boil in a large pot. Add the onions and cook them for 15 minutes, or until just tender. Drain and sprinkle with parsley, basil, and pepper.

SERVES 6

Braised White Onions

3 pounds small white onions
2 cups Vegetable Stock (see page 47)
3 tablespoons red wine vinegar
Bouquet garni (3 sprigs parsley, ¼ teaspoon thyme,
   ½ bay leaf)
¼ teaspoon freshly ground white pepper

Simmer all ingredients together for 1½ hours.
Remove bouquet garni before serving.

SERVES 6

Marinated Onions

2 Spanish onions, sliced
3 tablespoons lemon juice
1 tablespoon crushed dried mint
Romaine lettuce leaves

Toss all ingredients together and let them stand for
1½ hours.
Serve as an appetizer on lettuce leaves.

SERVES 6

Roasted Onions

6 medium onions, unpeeled
4 canned tomatoes, chopped
¼ cup Tomato Juice (see page 222)
1 teaspoon tarragon
½ teaspoon freshly ground black pepper
3 teaspoons white wine vinegar

Preheat oven to 330°F.
Place the onions in a baking pan and roast them for 1 ¾ hours, then peel.
Combine the tomatoes, tomato juice, tarragon, and pepper and cook over medium heat until the mixture thickens somewhat.
Add the vinegar and stir.
Arrange the onions on individual plates and pour the sauce over them.

SERVES 6

Stuffed Onions

6 large onions
6 cloves garlic
¼ cup lightly toasted whole-wheat bread crumbs
   (see page 151)
½ teaspoon freshly ground black pepper
¼ cup finely chopped parsley

Preheat oven to 400°F.
Blanch onions and garlic for 10 minutes. Hollow out centers of onions. Combine garlic, bread crumbs, and pepper with onion pulp and, in a mortar, pound to a paste with a pestle.
Mix with parsley, stuff onions, and bake in a 400°F oven for 15 minutes.

SERVES 6

Sweet-and-Sour White Onions

30 small white onions
¼ cup orange juice concentrate
¼ cup white wine vinegar
½ teaspoon freshly ground black pepper
¼ cup chopped parsley

Trim the ends of the onions and peel off the dry skins.

Combine the orange juice concentrate, the vinegar, pepper, and 1 cup of water in a skillet. Add the onions and bring to a simmer.

Cover tightly and cook slowly for 1 hour, adding more water as needed.

Sprinkle with parsley and serve.

SERVES 6

Green Peas with Dill

3 pounds unshelled peas
¼ teaspoon freshly ground black pepper
¼ cup chopped dill

Bring 2½ cups of water to boil. Add the peas and cook, uncovered, for 10 minutes or until just tender. Drain and add pepper and dill.
For an interesting alternative, these can be combined with Sweet-and-Sour White Onions (see page 91).

SERVES 6

Peas and Chickpeas with Turmeric

½ cup dried chickpeas
1 10-ounce package frozen peas
1 large onion, finely chopped
2 tablespoons turmeric
¼ teaspoon freshly ground black pepper
½ teaspoon thyme
Juice of 1 lemon

Place the chickpeas in a pot with water to cover and bring to a boil. Continue cooking them for 2 minutes, then cover and let stand for 1 hour. Simmer them until tender, then drain.

Place the frozen peas in a colander and run warm water over them to remove all the ice. Drain well.

In a large nonstick skillet, cook the onion and turmeric in ¼ cup water until soft. Add the pepper and thyme and cook 1 minute more.

Stir in the cooked chickpeas and lemon juice and cook for 5 minutes. Add the green peas and heat through.

SERVES 6

Stuffed Green Peppers

1 large eggplant, peeled and cut into ½-inch cubes
Salt
2 cloves garlic, minced
1 onion, finely chopped
⅓ cup canned tomatoes, chopped
1 tablespoon fresh basil, chopped (or 1 teaspoon dried)
1 tablespoon parsley, finely chopped
¼ teaspoon freshly ground black pepper
½ cup whole-wheat bread crumbs (see page 151)
6 green peppers, tops removed and seeded

Preheat the oven to 375°F.

Place the eggplant in a colander, sprinkle with salt, and toss. Place the colander in a bowl and refrigerate for 1 hour. Rinse the eggplant cubes very well and dry them with paper towels.

Brown the cubes lightly in a nonstick skillet, then remove them to a bowl. Add 2 tablespoons water to the skillet, then the garlic and onion, and cook until the onion is soft. Add the tomatoes and simmer for 5 minutes.

Add the basil, parsley, and pepper. Add the eggplant cubes and bread crumbs and heat them through.

Fill the peppers with the eggplant mixture and arrange them in a baking dish. Bake for 30 minutes.

SERVES 6

Stuffed Red Peppers

3 sweet potatoes
¼ teaspoon freshly ground black pepper
3 scallions, finely chopped (including green part)
¼ teaspoon grated lemon peel
4 sweet red peppers, tops removed and seeded
Finely chopped parsley (for garnish)

Preheat the oven to 325°F.
Peel the sweet potatoes and cut them into pieces.
Boil them until tender and push through a strainer.
Add the black pepper, scallions, and lemon peel and mix well.
Stuff the peppers with this mixture and arrange them in a nonstick baking pan.
Bake for 30 minutes.
Sprinkle with parsley and serve.

SERVES 6

Sweet Peppers à la Grecque

2 red bell peppers, halved and seeded
3 green bell peppers, halved and seeded
Juice of 1 lemon
1 tablespoon white wine vinegar
1 clove garlic
1 bay leaf
½ teaspoon freshly ground black pepper
1 teaspoon tarragon
1 tablespoon finely chopped parsley

Cut peppers into strips ½ inch wide. Combine with other ingredients, plus 1 cup water, in a saucepan.
Cover and bring to a boil.
Remove from heat, let mixture cool, and refrigerate.
Discard bay leaf before serving.

SERVES 6

Pamela's Potatoes and Cucumbers

1 pound red boiling potatoes, peeled and sliced
¼ teaspoon freshly ground black pepper
1 large basil leaf, roughly chopped
1 bay leaf
4 canned tomatoes
2 chilled cucumbers, peeled and quartered
     lengthwise

Combine ingredients, except for cucumbers, in a pot, barely cover with water, cover, and boil gently for 20 minutes.
When potatoes are tender, remove from heat. Discard bay leaf.
Add cucumbers just before serving.

SERVES 6

Potatoes with Garlic

6 baking potatoes, scrubbed
4 cloves garlic
1 teaspoon Dijon mustard
¼ teaspoon freshly ground white pepper
1 tablespoon tarragon vinegar
½ cup Mock Sour Cream (see page 206)

Preheat oven to 400°F.
Bake the potatoes until done (about 1 hour).
Mash the garlic to a paste with a mortar and pestle.
Mash in the mustard and pepper, then stir in the vinegar and sour cream.
When the potatoes are done, mash them in their skins.
Place a dollop of the sauce on each and serve.

SERVES 6

Hashed Brown Potatoes

½ onion, grated
3 cups chopped cooked potatoes
1 ½ tablespoons unbleached flour
⅓ cup skim milk
¼ cup chopped parsley

*Cook the onion with ¼ cup water until it is soft.
Mix the potatoes, flour, and onion. Add the skim milk and
mix well.*
*Place the potato mixture in a nonstick skillet and cook
gently until the bottom browns.*
Turn the potatoes and brown the other side.
Garnish with parsley and serve.

SERVES 6

Potatoes with Juniper Berries

1 ½ pounds potatoes, peeled and coarsely grated
¼ teaspoon freshly ground black pepper
1 red bell pepper, seeded and diced
6 crushed juniper berries

*Place potatoes in a colander and rinse well under
cold running water. Do not drain, but place them in a
skillet with other ingredients.*
*Cook gently, turning occasionally, for ½ hour. Add water
sparingly, as needed.*

SERVES 6

Saffron Potatoes

1 pound medium boiling potatoes, peeled
3 medium carrots, peeled
3 shallots, peeled
3 tablespoons finely chopped parsley
Pinch of saffron
½ teaspoon freshly ground black pepper

Boil potatoes and carrots separately in water to cover until almost done — potatoes, 20 minutes; carrots 15 minutes. Drain, reserving ¼ cup liquid from carrots. Cut potatoes into 1-inch dice, carrots into ¼-inch rounds. Heat reserved liquid in a skillet, add other ingredients, and cook, stirring, for 5 minutes.

SERVES 6

Steamed Potatoes

2 pounds small new potatoes, well scrubbed
½ teaspoon chopped basil or mint

Place potatoes on the rack of a steamer over boiling salted water. Cover and cook for 30 minutes, or until potatoes feel tender when pierced with a fork. Sprinkle with chopped basil or mint and serve.

SERVES 6

Stuffed Potatoes

6 baking potatoes, scrubbed
3 shallots, minced
6 mushrooms, minced
3 tablespoons tomato purée
1 medium zucchini, diced small
⅛ teaspoon cayenne
3 tablespoons fine whole-wheat bread crumbs
  (see page 151)

Preheat oven to 375°F.
Cut a thick slice off the top of each potato.
Scoop out the pulp of each, leaving a hollow shell. Set aside.
Boil the pulp for 15 to 20 minutes.
Drain well and mash with a fork.
Heat ¼ cup water in a skillet, add shallots and mushrooms, and cook until soft. Add tomato purée, zucchini, mashed potatoes, and cayenne and mix thoroughly. Stuff the potatoes and place in a baking dish. Sprinkle with bread crumbs and bake for 35 minutes. (During cooking, add a little water as necessary to prevent sticking.)

SERVES 6

Ratatouille

1 large eggplant, peeled and cut into 1-inch cubes
3 zucchini, cut into ¼-inch rounds
Salt
¼ cup white wine vinegar
2 medium onions, finely chopped
½ cup canned tomatoes, roughly chopped
2 cloves garlic, mashed
1 bay leaf
1 teaspoon thyme
¼ teaspoon freshly ground black pepper
2 red bell peppers, cut into ¼-inch-wide strips
½ cup chopped fresh basil (or parsley) for garnish

Put the eggplant cubes and the zucchini in a colander, sprinkle with salt, and toss well. Place the colander in a bowl and refrigerate for 30 minutes. Rinse well to wash off all the salt, and dry well.

Place 1 tablespoon vinegar, the onions, tomatoes, garlic, bay leaf, ½ teaspoon thyme, and pepper in a skillet and cook gently for 10 minutes.

Cook the eggplant in a nonstick skillet with ¼ cup water for 5 minutes.

Do the same with the zucchini, then the red peppers.

Combine everything, including ½ teaspoon thyme, except the basil and simmer, uncovered, for ½ hour. Garnish with basil (or parsley) and serve hot or chilled.

SERVES 6

Rutabaga Purée

3 medium rutabagas, peeled and diced
2 medium potatoes, peeled and diced
¼ teaspoon freshly ground white pepper
½ teaspoon freshly ground nutmeg
¼ cup chopped parsley (for garnish)

Place the rutabagas and potatoes in a pot with water to barely cover.
Bring the water to a boil, cover, and boil gently for 25 to 30 minutes.
Drain well and purée the rutabagas and potatoes through a food mill into a bowl. Add the pepper and nutmeg, stirring them in gently.
Garnish with parsley.

SERVES 6

Spinach and Mushrooms

2 pounds fresh spinach
½ onion, chopped
2 cloves garlic, minced
1 pound mushrooms, sliced
¼ teaspoon cayenne pepper
1 tablespoon soy sauce
¼ cup grated sapsago cheese

Wash the spinach well and do not dry it.
Cook the onion in ¼ cup water until soft.
Add the garlic and mushrooms and cook over medium heat, stirring, for 2 minutes.
Place the damp spinach in a pot. Cover and cook until it wilts. Drain it well, chop roughly, and add it to the mushroom mixture.
Add the pepper and soy sauce, stir, and place the spinach mixture in a nonstick baking dish.
Sprinkle cheese over the spinach and place under the broiler to brown the top.

SERVES 6

Spinach with Yogurt

3 pounds fresh spinach leaves, trimmed
½ cup Low-Fat Yogurt (see page 207)
Peel of 2 lemons
¼ teaspoon freshly ground black pepper
2 tablespoons lemon juice
¼ teaspoon crushed clove

Wash spinach well. Put the still-wet leaves in a large pot and cook over medium-high heat, stirring occasionally, until they wilt. Squeeze out excess water and reserve. Roughly chop the spinach.
Heat 3 tablespoons of water from the spinach in a skillet. Add spinach and reheat. Add other ingredients and stir well.

SERVES 6

Baked Summer Squash

1 onion, finely chopped
2 cloves garlic, minced
1 green pepper, seeded and diced small
¾ cup canned tomatoes, chopped
3 tablespoons finely chopped parsley
½ teaspoon freshly ground black pepper
1½ pounds summer squash, peeled and cut into
   1-inch cubes

Preheat oven to 350°F.
Place ¼ cup water in a skillet with the chopped onion and cook until the onion is soft. Add the garlic and green pepper and cook 3 to 4 minutes more.
Add the tomatoes, parsley, and black pepper and cook over medium heat for 10 minutes, stirring occasionally.
Bring ½ cup water to a boil in a saucepan. Add squash cubes and cover. Cook until the squash is just tender, then drain it well.
Place half the squash in a small nonstick casserole.
Spread half the tomato mixture over it, then make another layer of squash and another of tomato.
Bake 15 to 20 minutes.

SERVES 6

Baked Sweet Potatoes

6 sweet potatoes
Cinnamon or nutmeg, to taste

Preheat oven to 425°F.
Scrub potatoes. Place in oven and bake for 40 minutes.
Halfway through, pierce potatoes with a fork to let steam
escape.
Open and sprinkle with cinnamon or nutmeg.

SERVES 6

Boiled Sweet Potatoes

4 medium sweet potatoes, washed and quartered
Water to cover

Bring water to boil. Add potatoes and cook, cov-
ered, 10 to 15 minutes, or until just tender when pierced
with a fork.
Drain and remove skins.

SERVES 6

Sweet Potato Purée

    4 medium sweet potatoes
    ¼ cup apple juice concentrate
    ⅛ teaspoon powdered ginger
    ¼ teaspoon freshly ground black pepper
    ¼ teaspoon cinnamon
    ⅛ teaspoon ground clove

*Peel the sweet potatoes and cut them into pieces.
Boil until tender and push them through a strainer.
Combine the apple juice concentrate, ginger, pepper, cinnamon, and clove and stir well.
Heat this mixture and beat it into the sweet potato purée with a wooden spoon.*

SERVES 6

Sweet Potato Soufflé

4 medium sweet potatoes, boiled and mashed
⅛ teaspoon nutmeg
¼ cup unsweetened apple juice concentrate
¼ teaspoon freshly ground black pepper
½ teaspoon grated lemon peel
2 egg whites

Preheat oven to 350°F.
Add nutmeg, apple juice, pepper, and lemon peel to potatoes and beat hard until fluffy.
Beat egg whites until stiff and fold into potato mixture.
Bake soufflé in a 7-inch nonstick baking pan for 35 minutes.

SERVES 6

Baked Tomatoes

3 tablespoons minced shallots
½ cup whole-wheat bread crumbs (see page 151)
3 cloves garlic, minced
¼ cup minced parsley
¼ teaspoon freshly ground black pepper
6 ripe, firm tomatoes, halved

Preheat the oven to 325°F.
Sauté the shallots in 2 tablespoons water until soft.
Add the bread crumbs, garlic, parsley, and pepper and mix well.
Gently press the seeds out of the tomatoes. Cook the tomatoes, cut side down, in a nonstick skillet over low heat for 5 minutes.
Fill the cavities of the tomatoes with bread-crumb mixture. Arrange the tomatoes in a nonstick baking dish and bake in the oven for 12 minutes.

SERVES 6

Broiled Tomatoes

6 ripe tomatoes
Freshly ground black pepper
⅓ cup whole-wheat bread crumbs (see page 151)
¼ cup mixed chopped parsley and basil

Cut tomatoes in half. Sprinkle with pepper and bread crumbs. Place in a broiling pan, cut side up.
Broil about 4 inches from heat source until crumbs turn brown.
Sprinkle on herbs and serve.

SERVES 6

Stewed Tomatoes

6 large tomatoes, skinned and seeded
½ teaspoon freshly ground black pepper
¼ cup fresh basil, roughly chopped
2 slices stale Whole-Wheat Bread, crumbled
   (see page 151)

Put tomatoes into ½-inch dice and place in a sauce-pan with the pepper. Cover and cook gently, stirring occasionally, for 5 minutes.
Add basil and cook 5 minutes more. Mix in bread crumbs and cook until tomatoes are soft.

SERVES 6

Stuffed Tomatoes I

6 medium tomatoes
6 tablespoons Low-Fat Cottage Cheese
    (see page 203)
⅔ cup Low-Fat Yogurt (see page 207)
2 tablespoons minced scallion
2 tablespoons finely chopped dill
2 cloves garlic, mashed
½ teaspoon freshly ground black pepper
3 cups fresh spinach, washed and not dried
Lettuce leaves (for garnish)

Cut tops off tomatoes and scoop out pulp.
Blend cottage cheese, yogurt, scallion, dill, garlic, and pepper. Set aside.
Place the damp spinach in a pot, cover, and cook over medium heat, stirring occasionally, until it wilts. Squeeze out as much water as possible and chop fine. Blend with cottage-cheese mixture and chill.
Fill tomatoes with cheese mixture and serve on lettuce leaves.

SERVES 6

Stuffed Tomatoes II

6 ripe tomatoes
½ cup Low-Fat Cottage Cheese (see page 203)
2 tablespoons grated sapsago cheese
1 tablespoon chopped chives
1 tablespoon lemon juice
3 dashes Tabasco
2 tablespoons finely chopped parsley (for garnish)
Boston lettuce leaves (for garnish)

Cut off the top third of tomatoes. Scoop out insides, leaving shell intact.
Combine cottage cheese, sapsago, chives, lemon juice, and Tabasco and mix well. Stuff tomato shells with this mixture. Sprinkle parsley over the top and serve on lettuce leaves.

SERVES 6

Tomatoes Stuffed with Eggplant

6 medium ripe tomatoes
2 eggplants, peeled and cubed
Salt
2 cloves garlic, mashed
2 tablespoons finely chopped chives
2 tablespoons chopped fresh basil
1 tablespoon lemon juice
⅛ teaspoon Tabasco
1 teaspoon soy sauce
2 tablespoons Low-Fat Yogurt (see page 207)

Cut the tops off the tomatoes, then, with a spoon, remove the pulp and seeds without breaking the skin. Place the eggplant cubes in a colander and sprinkle with salt. Let stand for 30 minutes, then squeeze out the liquid and rinse the cubes under cold water. Chop the eggplant fine and mix it with the garlic, chives, basil, lemon juice, Tabasco, soy sauce, and yogurt.
Stuff the tomatoes with this mixture and chill before serving.

SERVES 6

Turnips with Dill

2 teaspoons caraway seeds
6 white turnips, trimmed
¼ cup Mock Sour Cream (see page 206)
¼ teaspoon freshly ground black pepper
2 tablespoons finely chopped fresh dill
2 tablespoons lemon juice

Preheat the oven to 350°F.
Place the caraway seeds in a pot of cold water and bring
to a boil. Add the turnips and cook them for 10 minutes.
Drain off the water.
Peel the turnips and slice them ⅛ inch thick.
Arrange them in a baking pan and mix in the sour cream
and pepper.
Cover the turnips and bake them for 20 minutes.
Sprinkle on the dill and lemon juice and serve.

SERVES 6

Turnip and Rice Purée

1 bay leaf
1 cup skim milk mixed with 1 cup water
¾ cup brown rice
4 cloves garlic, mashed
¼ teaspoon thyme
¼ teaspoon freshly ground white pepper
4 white turnips, peeled and diced
¼ cup chopped parsley (for garnish)

*Place the bay leaf in a pot with the milk and water
and heat it to simmering.
Add the rice, garlic, thyme, and pepper and stir well.
Cover and simmer for 30 minutes.
Add the turnips and add water to cover. Cover the pot and
simmer another 15 minutes. Remove bay leaf.
Purée the mixture and garnish with parsley.*

SERVES 6

Vegetable Casserole

1 large eggplant, peeled and sliced
2 medium zucchini, sliced
2 large onions, minced
1 cup canned tomatoes, roughly chopped
2 tablespoons chopped fresh basil (or 1 teaspoon dried basil)
1 teaspoon thyme
½ teaspoon freshly ground black pepper
½ cup whole-wheat bread crumbs (see page 151)

Preheat oven to 325°F.

Salt the eggplant and zucchini and refrigerate for ½ hour. Rinse well.

Bring a potful of water to a boil and blanch the eggplant and zucchini for 5 minutes. Drain well.

Cook the onions in ¼ cup water until they are soft.

In a nonstick baking dish, place a layer of onion, then a layer of zucchini, a layer of tomato, and a layer of eggplant.

Sprinkle with some basil, thyme, and pepper. Repeat the layers.

Drain the excess liquid and reduce it to ¼ cup.

Sprinkle the bread crumbs over the vegetables and bake the casserole for 40 minutes.

SERVES 6

Watercress Sandwiches

Whites of 4 hard-cooked eggs, finely chopped
1 tablespoon Dijon mustard
2 tablespoons grated red onion
½ teaspoon red wine vinegar
¼ teaspoon freshly ground black pepper
6 thin slices of Whole-Wheat Bread, toasted and
    cut into triangles (see page 151)
2 bunches watercress, tough stems removed

Combine the egg whites, mustard, onion, vinegar, and pepper and mix well. Spread this mixture on half the pieces of toast and cover well with watercress.
Put the remaining triangles on top of the spread pieces to make sandwiches.

SERVES 6

Grated Zucchini with Fresh Basil

> 10 small zucchini
> Salt
> ¼ cup minced fresh basil or parsley
> Freshly ground black pepper to taste

Slice off stems and tips of zucchini. Grate coarsely and sprinkle liberally with salt. Place in a colander over a bowl for 30 minutes. Rinse thoroughly under cold running water. Use paper towels to squeeze out as much water as possible, reserving ¼ cup of the water extracted. Heat reserved water in a skillet and add zucchini, basil (or parsley), and pepper. Cook, tossing occasionally, until mixture is heated through.

SERVES 6

Stuffed Zucchini Boats

6 small zucchini, washed well, stems trimmed
4 scallions, finely chopped
3 cloves garlic, minced
1 tablespoon finely chopped parsley
½ cup canned tomatoes, drained and chopped
1 teaspoon marjoram
½ teaspoon oregano
⅓ cup whole-wheat bread crumbs (see page 151)

Preheat oven to 350°F.
Cut a ¼-inch slice lengthwise off each zucchini.
Scoop out the flesh, leaving the shells intact.
Finely chop the removed flesh and the sliced portion of the skin.
Heat ¼ cup water in a skillet. Gently cook the scallions, garlic, parsley, and chopped zucchini for 4 minutes.
In a mixing bowl, combine the tomatoes, marjoram, oregano, and zucchini mixture and stir well. Add bread crumbs and stir.
Fill the zucchini shells with the mixture and place with ¼ cup water in a baking dish.
Bake for ½ hour, basting occasionally with pan juices.

SERVES 6

LEGUMES

Because we don't eat meat on this diet, we do eat plenty of beans and lentils — high in protein and low in cost. Poor old Esau so valued legumes that he sold his birthright, as you may recall, for a mess of pottage, which was a stew of lentils and onions — and not nearly so tasty as what we have here.

Baked Beans

3 cups quick-cooking dried white pea beans
1 medium onion, peeled
¼ cup orange juice concentrate
1 tablespoon dry mustard
1 tablespoon tomato paste
1 ½ teaspoons freshly ground black pepper

Place beans in a pot with water to cover, bring to a boil, and simmer for 20 to 25 minutes. Drain them well. Preheat the oven to 250°F.
Combine the beans with all the other ingredients in a bean pot. Add boiling water to cover, cover the pot, and bake in the oven for 4 hours, adding boiling water as needed.
Remove the cover and cook the beans ½ hour more without adding water.

SERVES 6

Black Beans with Celery

1 pound dried black beans
6 cups water
2 onions, chopped
3 cloves garlic, minced
2 ribs celery, sliced thin
1 carrot, finely chopped
Bouquet garni (1 bay leaf, ½ teaspoon thyme,
    4 sprigs parsley)
Freshly ground black pepper
6 tablespoons red wine vinegar
1 tablespoon soy sauce

Boil beans for 2 minutes in water to cover, then soak 1 hour. Drain and add 6 cups water. Combine all ingredients except vinegar and soy sauce.
Simmer slowly until beans are just tender. Remove bouquet garni.
Place beans and liquid in a casserole and add vinegar and soy sauce. Cover and bake in a 350°F oven for 2 hours.

SERVES 6

Black Beans with Lemon

1 pound dried black beans
1 medium onion, minced
⅛ teaspoon chili powder
½ teaspoon freshly ground black pepper
¼ cup minced parsley
1 clove garlic, minced
¼ cup lemon juice

Place the beans in a pot with water to cover and bring to a boil. Continue cooking them for 2 minutes, then cover and let stand for 1 hour. Simmer the beans until tender, then drain them.

Cook the onion and the chili powder in ¼ cup water until the onion is soft. Add the pepper, parsley, garlic, and lemon juice, and cook gently for 5 minutes. Add the beans and heat them through.

SERVES 6

124.

Chickpeas with Herbs

1 ½ pounds dried chickpeas, soaked overnight
    and drained
1 onion, stuck with a clove
1 carrot, minced
1 clove garlic
Bouquet garni (1 bay leaf, ½ teaspoon thyme,
    4 sprigs parsley)
½ teaspoon freshly ground black pepper
Juice of ½ lemon
¼ cup minced parsley

Combine everything except parsley and lemon with water to cover. Bring to a boil and simmer until chickpeas are tender (about 1 hour).
Remove onion and bouquet garni; drain chickpeas.
Sprinkle with lemon juice and parsley, mix, and serve.

SERVES 6

Chili

½ pound dried kidney beans
½ pound dried pinto beans
1 large onion, finely chopped
1 rib celery, finely chopped
3 cloves garlic, minced
1 ½ teaspoons paprika
1 ½ tablespoons chili powder
½ teaspoon cumin
1 teaspoon oregano
2 cups canned tomatoes
1 tablespoon tomato paste
⅛ teaspoon Tabasco
¼ teaspoon freshly ground black pepper
2 tablespoons soy sauce

Place the beans in a pot with water to cover and bring to a boil. Continue cooking them for 2 minutes, then cover and let stand for 1 hour. Drain, reserving ¾ cup of liquid.

Combine all ingredients (including that liquid) in a large pot, bring to a simmer and cook gently for 5 hours.

SERVES 6

Boiled Great Northern Beans

1½ pounds dried Great Northern beans
1 onion stuck with 1 clove
2 cloves garlic
1 rib celery
Bouquet garni (1 bay leaf, ½ teaspoon thyme,
   4 sprigs parsley)

Combine all ingredients with water to cover. Bring to a boil and boil 2 minutes. Allow to stand 1 hour, then cook beans until tender (about 40 minutes).
Remove bouquet garni and serve.

SERVES 6

Great Northern Beans Provençale

1 pound dried Great Northern beans
2 onions, finely chopped
2 cloves garlic, minced
6 canned tomatoes, chopped
½ teaspoon thyme
1 teaspoon freshly ground black pepper
¼ cup chopped parsley (for garnish)

Cover beans with water and bring to a boil. Cook 2 minutes. Cover and let stand 1 hour. Simmer until tender. Drain.

Sauté onions and garlic in 3 tablespoons water until onions are soft. Add tomatoes, thyme, and pepper and cook 5 minutes, stirring.

Pour beans into serving dish and top with tomato sauce. Garnish with parsley.

SERVES 6

Hummus

1 pound dried chickpeas, soaked overnight
2 cloves garlic, mashed
¼ cup lemon juice
Cayenne pepper
¼ cup chopped parsley

Cover the chickpeas with cold water, bring to a boil, and simmer for 2 hours.
Purée the chickpeas with the garlic, lemon juice, and as much of the water in which they were cooked as necessary.
Season with cayenne pepper to taste.
Garnish the hummus with parsley and serve with raw vegetables or whole-wheat pita bread.

SERVES 6

Kidney Beans Kraus

2 pounds dried kidney beans
3 cloves garlic, peeled
½ teaspoon thyme
1 bay leaf
½ teaspoon freshly ground black pepper
¼ cup red wine vinegar
2 cups Vegetable Stock (see page 47)
2 onions, sliced
4 carrots, peeled and cut into ½-inch rounds
1 rib celery, diced very small
3 ripe tomatoes, cut into wedges

*Combine the beans with the garlic, thyme, bay
leaf, pepper, vinegar, and stock plus water to cover.
Bring the liquid to a boil and cook for 2 minutes.
Allow to rest 1 hour.
Add the onions, carrots, and celery and cook the beans
until they are almost tender.
Add the tomatoes and cook a few minutes more.
Remove bay leaf before serving.*

SERVES 6

Aunt Harriet's Lentils

1 ½ cups dried lentils, washed and drained
2 small onions, finely chopped
3 cloves garlic, minced
1 teaspoon ground cumin
1 cup canned tomatoes, chopped, with juice
¼ teaspoon freshly ground black pepper
1 tablespoon red wine vinegar

Simmer the lentils in water to cover for 1 hour, or until they are just tender. Drain and set aside.
In a large saucepan, cook the onions and garlic with ¼ cup water until the onions are soft.
Add the cumin, tomatoes, and pepper and cook a few minutes more.
Add the lentils, stir, and heat through.
Add the vinegar, stir, and serve.

SERVES 6

Farmhouse Lentils

2 medium onions, finely chopped
1 tablespoon unbleached flour
2 cups Vegetable Stock (see page 47)
Bouquet garni (1 bay leaf, a pinch thyme, 1 strip
   dried orange peel, 3 sprigs parsley)
1 clove garlic
2 tablespoons tomato paste
½ teaspoon freshly ground black pepper
3 cups dried lentils, washed and drained

*Sauté onions in 3 tablespoons water. Add flour and
allow to brown lightly, stirring constantly.*
*Add other ingredients, stir, and simmer gently until lentils
are tender.*
Remove the bouquet garni and serve.

SERVES 6

Priscilla's Lentil Stew

3 medium onions, finely chopped
2 carrots, finely chopped
1 green pepper, seeded and chopped
3 cloves garlic, minced
½ teaspoon thyme
¼ teaspoon oregano
¼ teaspoon basil
¼ teaspoon freshly ground black pepper
1 2-pound, 3-ounce can of tomatoes, with juice
2 cups lentils, washed and drained

In a large pot cook the onions in ½ cup of water until they are translucent.

Add the carrots, green pepper, garlic, thyme, oregano, basil, pepper, and tomato (with juice) and simmer for 15 minutes.

Add the lentils and ½ cup water and simmer gently for 1 hour.

SERVES 6

Oriental Lentils

6 cups water
2 cups dried lentils, washed and drained
1 stick cinnamon
1 bay leaf
5 cloves garlic
¼ teaspoon powdered ginger
1 teaspoon turmeric
3 tablespoons lemon juice
¼ teaspoon freshly ground black pepper

Combine all the ingredients, bring to a boil, cover, and simmer gently for 45 minutes.
Remove cinnamon, bay leaf, and garlic before serving.

SERVES 6

Lima Beans Entomatado

3 cups dried lima beans
2 medium onions, finely chopped
2 pounds canned tomatoes
2 cloves garlic, mashed
2 tablespoons tomato paste
2 tablespoons chopped fresh basil (or 2 teaspoons dried basil)
1 tablespoon red wine vinegar
¼ cup chopped parsley (for garnish)

Cover the beans with cold water and bring to a boil. Cook for 2 minutes, turn off the heat, and let the beans stand for 1 hour. Cook them until they are tender.
Cook the onions in ¼ cup water until they are soft.
Add the tomatoes, garlic, tomato paste, and basil and simmer, stirring, for 10 minutes. Add the vinegar, stir, and pour the sauce over the beans.
Garnish with parsley.

SERVES 6

Savory Lima Beans

1 pound dried lima beans
2 teaspoons savory
¼ teaspoon freshly ground black pepper
2 tablespoons lemon juice
¼ cup chopped parsley

Combine the lima beans and savory with cold water to cover. Bring to a boil and cook for 2 minutes. Let the beans stand for 1 hour, then simmer until they are tender. Drain the beans and combine them with the other ingredients. Stir and serve.

SERVES 6

GRAINS

O beautiful for spacious skies, for amber waves of grain — which means rice, groats, and barley, too. Rice has a major role in this book; it is very versatile. And its story should be told. Rice started out brown. Then, around the turn of the century, when Victorians were covering naked piano legs with paisley shawls, somebody decided that brown rice looked dirty and should be made white. The protein and natural oil were removed, as were the vitamins and minerals. White-rice eaters died promptly of beriberi. Today's converted rice has thiamine, iron, and vitamins shot back into it, which is ridiculous. So we use brown rice, as God meant us to. It is healthy, nutty-tasting, and available in short, medium, and long grain.

Barley Casserole

2 medium onions, chopped
1 green pepper, seeded and diced
2 cups pearl barley
½ teaspoon freshly ground black pepper
3 cups boiling Vegetable Stock (see page 47)

Preheat oven to 300°F.

Heat ¼ cup water in a skillet and add onions. Cook 2 minutes and add green pepper.

Place onions and green pepper with barley and ground black pepper in a heavy casserole and stir.

Add half the stock, cover, and bake in preheated oven for 45 minutes.

Add remaining stock, cover, and bake 45 minutes more.

SERVES 6

Barley and Mushrooms

2 onions, finely chopped
3 cloves garlic, minced
1 pound mushrooms, thinly sliced
1 tablespoon chopped fresh basil
1 cup pearl barley, washed and drained
1 ½ cups Vegetable Stock (see page 47)
¼ teaspoon freshly ground black pepper
3 tablespoons chopped fresh parsley

Preheat oven to 325°F.
Cook the onions in a pot with ¼ cup water until soft.
Add the garlic, mushrooms, and basil and cook gently for 5 minutes more.
Add the barley and stir well.
Add the stock and the pepper and stir well.
Bring the liquid to a boil, stir again, cover, and bake in the oven for 45 minutes.
Sprinkle with parsley and serve.

SERVES 6

Croutons

Slices whole-wheat bread (see page 151)

Remove the crusts from the bread with a serrated knife. Then cut each slice into four equal strips.
Cut each strip into four small squares.
Arrange the squares on a baking pan and toast under the broiler until they are lightly browned (be careful — it doesn't take much to burn them). Then turn the bread and toast the other side.

Kasha

1½ cups buckwheat groats
2 egg whites
2 cups Vegetable Stock (see page 47)
¼ teaspoon freshly ground black pepper
1 tablespoon soy sauce

Mix the groats and egg whites thoroughly in a skillet.
Cook the mixture over medium heat, stirring, until it is dry.
Add the stock, pepper, and soy sauce, stir, cover, lower the heat, and simmer the groats for 30 minutes or until the liquid is absorbed.

SERVES 6

Polenta

1 ½ quarts water
1 pound cornmeal
2 cups Tomato Sauce (see pages 175–176)

Bring water to a boil. Pour cornmeal in slowly, stirring constantly with a wooden spoon, and cook, still stirring, for ½ hour (or until cornmeal no longer sticks to sides of the pan).
Pour mush into a mold, cover, and steam over hot water until it firms up (about 3 hours).
Serve with tomato sauce.

SERVES 6

Rice and Beans

¾ cup dried navy beans
2 onions, chopped
1 rib celery, chopped
2 cups canned tomatoes
2 dashes Tabasco
¾ cup brown rice
2 tablespoons grated sapsago cheese

*Place beans in water to cover. Bring to a boil for
2 minutes and then soak 1 hour. Simmer until tender,
adding water if necessary.*
*Add onions, celery, tomatoes, Tabasco, rice, and water
to cover. Cover pot and cook, stirring frequently, until
rice is done (about 45 minutes), adding water if necessary.
Sprinkle with cheese and serve.*

SERVES 6

Rice Casserole Entomatado

> 2 onions, chopped
> 2 cloves garlic, minced
> ½ cup sliced mushrooms
> 1 ½ cups brown rice
> 2 ½ cups tomato juice
> 2 cups boiling Vegetable Stock (see page 47)
> ¼ teaspoon freshly ground black pepper
> ¼ cup grated sapsago cheese

Heat ¼ cup water in a saucepan. Add onions, garlic, and mushrooms and cook, stirring, for 5 minutes. Add the rice, 2 cups of the tomato juice, stock, and pepper and simmer, covered, until the liquid has been absorbed (about 45 minutes).

Remove rice to a 1-quart casserole. Pour the remaining ½ cup of tomato juice over the top and sprinkle with cheese. Place under broiler until cheese browns.

SERVES 6

Curried Rice

4 cups Vegetable Stock, boiling (see page 47)
1 large onion, minced
4 tablespoons curry powder
⅛ teaspoon saffron
4 tablespoons tomato paste
1½ cups brown rice
1 bay leaf

Place ¼ cup of the stock in a saucepan with the onion and cook until the onion is soft. Add the curry powder and saffron, stir, and cook over medium heat for 1 minute. Stir in the tomato paste.
Add the rice, mix, and then pour in the boiling stock.
Add the bay leaf and stir well. Bring stock to a second boil, stir again, cover and reduce to a simmer.
Cook for 45 minutes. Remove bay leaf before serving.

SERVES 6

Herbed Rice

1 teaspoon thyme
2 bay leaves
1 ½ cups brown rice
¼ teaspoon freshly ground black pepper
¼ cup mixed parsley and dill, finely chopped

Place the thyme and bay leaves in 4 cups cold water and bring to a boil. Add the rice, stir well, and cover.
When it returns to a boil, stir it again, cover and cook for 45 minutes.
Drain the rice in a colander, remove the bay leaves, and mix in the pepper and chopped herbs.

SERVES 6

Rice with Mushrooms

3 ¼ cups water
2 cups dried mushrooms
2 cloves garlic, minced
2 dashes Tabasco
2 cloves
1 small onion, thinly sliced
1 ½ cups brown rice

Soak the mushrooms in 3 ¼ cups cold water for 2 hours.
Add the garlic, Tabasco, cloves, and onion and bring to a boil.
Add the rice, stir, return to the boil, stir again, cover and simmer for 45 minutes.

SERVES 6

Rice Pilaf

2 small onions, peeled
4 cups boiling Vegetable Stock (see page 47)
1 ½ cups brown rice
1 clove
1 bay leaf
¼ teaspoon freshly ground black pepper
2 tablespoons soy sauce

Finely chop 1 of the onions and cook it with ¼ cup of the vegetable stock until it is soft.
Add the rice and stir.
Stick the clove into the other onion. Add with the bay leaf and pepper to the rice. Add the boiling stock and the soy sauce and stir.
Bring the stock to a second boil, stir again, cover the pot, and lower heat to a simmer.
Cook for 45 minutes. Remove bay leaf before serving.

SERVES 6

Saffron Rice

2 pinches saffron
3 ¾ cups Vegetable Stock (see page 47)
1 ½ cups brown rice
¼ teaspoon freshly ground black pepper

Combine the saffron with the stock and bring it to a boil.

Add the rice, stir it, and allow the stock to come to a second boil.

Stir again, cover the pot, and simmer for 45 minutes or until all the liquid is absorbed.

SERVES 6

Spanish Rice

1 large onion, finely chopped
1 large clove garlic, minced
2 cups canned tomatoes, chopped
¼ pound mushrooms, cut in wedges
1 cup shelled peas
2 red bell peppers, seeded and diced
2 tablespoons soy sauce
¼ teaspoon freshly ground black pepper
1 tablespoon chopped cilantro (fresh coriander)
1 ½ cups brown rice, cooked

Cook the onion with ¼ cup water until it is soft. Add the garlic, tomatoes, mushrooms, peas, red peppers, soy sauce, and pepper and cook gently, stirring occasionally until the peas are done.
Stir in the cilantro and combine the mixture with the rice. Toss and serve.

SERVES 6

Tabouli

    1 cup bulgar (cracked wheat)
    8 scallions, chopped
    ¼ cup finely chopped parsley
    ¼ cup chopped fresh mint
    3 ripe tomatoes, peeled and chopped
    ¼ cup lemon juice
    ¼ teaspoon freshly ground black pepper
    6 large Boston lettuce leaves

Place the bulgar in a bowl with water to cover. Allow it to soak 15 minutes, then drain and squeeze it dry. Combine all the ingredients except the lettuce in a mixing bowl and mix well.
Serve the tabouli on individual leaves.

SERVES 6

Whole-Wheat Bread

2 ¼ cups skim milk
1 envelope dry active yeast
6 cups stone-ground whole-wheat flour

*Heat ¼ cup milk to lukewarm. Stir in the yeast
and let it stand about 5 minutes.*
*Warm the remaining milk to between 100°F and 115°F.
Place it in a bowl and stir in the flour, 1 cup at a time, with
a wooden spoon.*
*Add the yeast mixture after the third cup of flour, then
continue adding the rest of the flour.*
*Knead the dough on a heavily floured board until it is no
longer sticky. Place it in a floured bowl, cover, and allow
it to rise for 1 ½ hours.*
*Divide the dough in half and shape the halves into two
loaves. Put these into nonstick loaf pans, cover, and allow
them to rise for 1 hour more.*
Meanwhile, preheat the oven to 400°F.
*Bake the loaves for 45 minutes, or until the loaves sound
hollow when tapped on the bottom.*
Allow the loaves to cool on a rack.

YIELD: 2 loaves

PASTAS

One theory has it that pasta, like aqueducts and emperors, originated in Rome. Another has it that Marco Polo brought pasta back to Italy from China. Another has it that the Arabs and Indians were twirling their own edible "thread" years earlier. However noodles came about, they were well established in Europe by the eighteenth century, which led eventually to Yankee Doodle's liking for macaroni, which leads to the recipes below. Pasta — in all its shapes — is marvelously versatile, satisfying, nutritious (containing protein, iron, amino acids, vitamins, and minerals), and, on this diet, not even fattening! Jonathan gives recipes for spinach pasta dough and whole-wheat pasta dough here; if you prefer spaghetti of a lighter hue, however, there is pasta made of Jerusalem artichoke flour available in health-food stores.

Spinach Pasta Dough

1 10-ounce package frozen spinach, thawed
1 ½ cups Jerusalem artichoke flour
3 egg whites, lightly beaten

Squeeze as much liquid as possible out of the spinach.
Chop it very fine.
Pour the flour in a mound and make a hollow in the center.
Combine the egg whites and spinach in the hollow and slowly work in the flour until it forms a fairly smooth mass.
Knead the dough with the heels of your hands for 10 minutes.
Wrap the dough in plastic and let it rest in the refrigerator for 1 hour.
Roll the dough to a thin sheet on a floured surface.
Allow it to sit for 30 minutes.
Fold the sheet of pasta very loosely into a cylindrical roll.
Cut the pasta to the width desired.

Note: *Fresh pasta needs less cooking than packaged pasta, so cook in plenty of boiling water for only 4 minutes or so.*

SERVES 6

Whole-Wheat Pasta Dough

1 cup whole-wheat flour
2 egg whites, lightly beaten
1 tablespoon skim milk

Heap the flour in a mound and scoop out a hollow in the center.
Combine the whites and the milk and pour them into the hollow.
Little by little, combine the flour and egg-white mixture, working it with your hands, until it forms a smooth paste.
Knead the dough with the heels of your hands for 10 minutes.
Wrap the dough in plastic and let it rest in the refrigerator for 1 hour.
Roll the dough to a thin sheet on a floured surface.
Allow it to sit for 30 minutes.
Fold the sheet of pasta very loosely into a cylindrical shape.
Cut the pasta to the width desired.

Note: *Fresh pasta needs less cooking than packaged pasta, so cook in plenty of boiling water for only 4 minutes or so.*

SERVES 6

Lasagna

> 1 pound whole-wheat or spinach lasagna (see pages
>   154–155)
> 3 cups Tomato Sauce (see pages 175–176)
> 2 pounds Low-Fat Cottage Cheese (see page 203)

Preheat oven to 325°F.
Cook lasagna in plenty of boiling water until just tender.
Drain.
Cover the bottom of a nonstick baking dish with a thin
layer of tomato sauce. Arrange a layer of lasagna over it.
Dot with cottage cheese and spoon on tomato sauce. Con-
tinue with alternating layers until lasagna is all used, end-
ing with a cheese-and-sauce layer on top.
Bake 20 minutes.

SERVES 6

Stuffed Manicotti

½ pound whole-wheat manicotti (see page 155)
2 onions, chopped
3 cloves garlic, minced
1 pound mushrooms, chopped
1 cup Low-Fat Cottage Cheese (see page 203)
½ cup whole-wheat bread crumbs (see page 151)
2 egg whites, slightly beaten
¼ teaspoon oregano
¼ teaspoon freshly ground black pepper
3 cups Tomato Sauce (see pages 175–176)
½ cup grated sapsago cheese (optional)

Bring a large quantity of water to a boil. Add pasta, cooking 8 minutes. Drain and rinse under cold water. Set aside.

Preheat oven to 350°F.

Heat ¼ cup water in a skillet. Add onions and cook until soft. Add garlic and continue cooking until onions are lightly browned. Add mushrooms and cook 3 minutes. Blend this mixture with cottage cheese, bread crumbs, egg whites, oregano, and pepper. With a teaspoon, stuff the pasta.

Spread a thin layer of tomato sauce over the bottom of a shallow rectangular casserole. Arrange a layer of stuffed manicotti on top, cover with more sauce and, if desired, sprinkle with sapsago. Repeat the layers.

Bake for ½ hour.

SERVES 6

Pasta à la Chinoise

1½ pounds whole-wheat or spinach macaroni
  (see pages 154–155)
½ cup soy sauce mixed with ¼ cup of water
2 teaspoons finely chopped fresh ginger
2 cloves garlic, minced
5 scallions, thinly sliced
2 tablespoons rice vinegar

Bring plenty of water to a boil and cook the macaroni until just tender. Drain in a colander and rinse thoroughly with cold water. Drain again and set aside.
Mix the other ingredients.
Place the macaroni in a bowl and toss with the sauce to serve.

SERVES 6

Pasta e Fagioli

> 1 pound dried pinto beans
> Vegetable Stock to cover (see page 47)
> 1 onion, chopped
> ½ cup sliced celery
> ¼ cup chopped carrot
> 2 teaspoons chopped parsley
> ½ cup canned tomatoes
> ½ teaspoon freshly ground black pepper
> 2 cups whole-wheat or spinach macaroni (see pages 154–155)

Boil beans in stock for 2 minutes. Cover the pot and let stand for 2 hours.

Add onion, celery, carrot, parsley, and tomato and simmer, uncovered, for 2 hours. Add pepper.

Purée half the beans and return them to the pot.

Cook pasta in plenty of boiling water until just done.

Reheat beans and serve over the macaroni.

SERVES 6

Pasta Florentine

2 pounds fresh spinach, trimmed and washed well
1 pound whole-wheat or spinach macaroni
(see pages 154–155)
1 cup Low-Fat Cottage Cheese (see page 203)
1 tablespoon grated sapsago cheese
¼ teaspoon freshly ground black pepper

Cook the still-damp spinach in a covered pot until leaves wilt. Drain well, then squeeze out excess water. Finely chop the spinach.
Cook the macaroni in plenty of boiling water until just tender. Drain in a colander.
Transfer the pasta to a warmed serving bowl, adding spinach, cottage cheese, sapsago, and pepper.
Mix well and serve.

SERVES 6

Pasta with Mushrooms

2 shallots, finely chopped
1 clove garlic, minced
2 pounds mushrooms, sliced
½ teaspoon freshly ground black pepper
1 teaspoon chopped parsley
2 teaspoons chopped fresh basil
1 pound whole-wheat or spinach macaroni
  (see pages 154–155)
1 teaspoon lemon juice

Cook the shallots with ¼ cup water until they are soft. Add the garlic and mushrooms and cook for 10 minutes, adding water if necessary. Add the pepper, parsley, and basil and stir well.

Cook the macaroni in plenty of boiling water until it is just done. Drain well.

Pour the mushroom mixture plus lemon juice over the pasta, toss, and serve.

SERVES 6

Gnocchi in Tomato Sauce

3 medium baking potatoes
1 cup unbleached flour
2 cups Tomato Sauce (see pages 175–176)

Boil the potatoes until they can be pierced easily with a fork.
Drain them well, then peel and mash them.
Mix in the flour, kneading the dough until smooth.
Shape the dough into long rolls about as thick as your finger. Cut these into 1-inch pieces.
Put a large pot of water on to boil. Place a third of the gnocchi at one time in the pot. When they rise to the surface, remove them with a slotted spoon or a strainer and place them in a warm serving dish.
When all the gnocchi are cooked, add sauce and serve.

SERVES 6

Spaghetti with Eggplant

1 medium eggplant, peeled and cut into
   ½-inch cubes
Salt
½ cup thinly sliced onion
1 large clove garlic, minced
2 cups thin, ripe tomato wedges
½ teaspoon freshly ground black pepper
1 pound whole-wheat or spinach spaghetti
   (see pages 154–155)
1 tablespoon grated sapsago cheese
3 tablespoons Low-Fat Cottage Cheese
   (see page 203)
2 tablespoons chopped parsley

Place eggplant cubes in a colander and sprinkle liberally with salt. Allow to sit 1 hour in the sink. Rinse well to get out all the salt, then place cubes in a towel and squeeze out as much water as possible.

Cook cubes in a nonstick skillet over low to medium heat until tender. Remove eggplant and set aside.

Heat ¼ cup water in the skillet and cook onion until soft. Add garlic and cook 3 minutes more.

Add tomatoes and cook over medium heat for 10 minutes, stirring frequently. Add eggplant and pepper and cook, stirring, for 2 minutes.

Cook spaghetti in plenty of boiling water until just done. Drain and place in a warm bowl.

Stir in sauce, sapsago, cottage cheese, and parsley.

SERVES 6

Spaghetti Galli-Campi

3 large onions, chopped
5 cloves garlic, minced
½ red bell pepper, finely chopped
½ teaspoon freshly ground black pepper
½ teaspoon oregano
½ cup Mock Sour Cream (see page 206)
2 cups Low-Fat Cottage Cheese (see page 203)
1½ cups finely chopped parsley
1½ pounds whole-wheat or spinach spaghetti
   (see pages 154–155)

Heat ¼ cup water in a skillet. Add onions, garlic, and bell pepper and cook until onions are soft. Add ground pepper and oregano and cook 2 minutes more.
Add sour cream and stir, then add cottage cheese and heat until hot but not bubbling.
Stir in the parsley.
Cook spaghetti in plenty of boiling water, drain, and toss with sauce.

SERVES 6

Spaghetti with Fresh Herb Sauce

½ cup finely chopped parsley
½ cup finely chopped fresh basil
1 clove garlic, minced
2 tablespoons chopped scallion
1 ½ cups Low-Fat Cottage Cheese (see page 203)
¼ cup skim milk
¼ teaspoon freshly ground black pepper
1 ½ pounds whole-wheat or spinach spaghetti
(see pages 154–155)

Combine the parsley, basil, garlic, scallion, cottage cheese, milk, and pepper in a blender and blend until they make a smooth mixture.
Cook the spaghetti in plenty of boiling water until just tender.
Toss with the sauce and serve.

SERVES 6

Spaghetti Marinara

3 cloves garlic, minced
3 cups canned tomatoes
1 tablespoon chopped parsley
1 teaspoon basil
¼ teaspoon freshly ground black pepper
Large pinch of oregano
3 tablespoons tomato paste
1½ pounds whole-wheat or spinach spaghetti
   (see pages 154–155)

In a saucepan, cook garlic, tomatoes, parsley, basil, pepper, oregano, and tomato paste over medium heat, stirring, until sauce thickens (about 15 to 20 minutes).
Cook spaghetti until just done, drain, and place in a warm serving bowl. Pour on sauce and mix lightly.

SERVES 6

Spaghetti Mentonnaise

½ cup finely chopped shallots
1 green pepper, seeded and cut into thin strips
½ cup canned tomatoes, chopped
3 tablespoons tomato juice
½ cup Vegetable Stock (see page 47)
2 tablespoons white wine vinegar
¼ teaspoon freshly ground black pepper
3 tablespoons chopped fresh basil
⅛ teaspoon thyme
¾ pound whole-wheat or spinach spaghetti
  (see pages 154–155)

*Cook the shallots, green pepper, and tomatoes with
the tomato juice for 5 minutes, stirring continuously.
Add the stock, vinegar, pepper, basil, and thyme and cook
for 5 minutes.
Cook the spaghetti in plenty of boiling water, drain, and
toss with the sauce.*

SERVES 6

Baked Spaghetti and Tomato Sauce

1½ pounds whole-wheat or spinach spaghetti
   (see pages 154–155)
2 small onions, chopped
3 cloves garlic, minced
¾ cup chopped carrot
¾ cup chopped celery
1 green pepper, finely chopped
¾ pound mushrooms, chopped
½ teaspoon freshly ground black pepper
5 cups Tomato Sauce (see pages 175–176)
¼ cup grated sapsago cheese (optional)

Preheat oven to 350°F.
Cook spaghetti until just tender, drain, and arrange in a casserole.
Heat ½ cup water in a saucepan; add onions, garlic, carrot, celery, green pepper, and mushrooms. Cover and cook over low heat for 10 to 15 minutes (or until vegetables get soft), stirring occasionally.
Add pepper and tomato sauce and simmer 20 minutes.
Pour sauce over spaghetti and bake until top browns lightly. Serve with cheese.

SERVES 6

SAUCES

What's sauce for the goose is not sauce for the steamed asparagus, brown rice, whole-wheat linguine, or cauliflower. Thus, these recipes — despite the fact that Cervantes thought "there's no sauce in the world like hunger."

Asparagus Sauce

1 pound asparagus, peeled and cooked
½ cup Vegetable Stock (see page 47)
1 ½ teaspoons dry tarragon
1 tablespoon white wine vinegar
¼ teaspoon freshly ground white pepper
1 teaspoon Mock Sour Cream (see page 206)

Purée ingredients. Serve warm on steamed vegetables.

YIELD: 2 cups

Sauce Aurore

2 tablespoons tomato paste
2 tablespoons unbleached flour
1 cup Vegetable Stock, heated (see page 47)

In a saucepan blend the tomato paste and flour together.
Add ¼ cup of the stock and stir with a wire whisk until the mixture is smooth. Add the rest of the stock, beating continuously. Bring the mixture to a boil, lower to a simmer, and cook gently for 5 minutes.

YIELD: 1 ¼ cups

Curry Sauce

> 1 medium onion, chopped
> 1 clove garlic, minced
> 1 rib celery, cut into small dice
> 1 bay leaf
> ¼ teaspoon powdered mustard
> 2 tablespoons unbleached flour
> ½ teaspoon mace
> 1½ teaspoons curry powder
> 2½ cups Vegetable Stock (see page 47)

Combine onion, garlic, celery, bay leaf, and mustard and cook in ½ cup water for 10 minutes, stirring occasionally.

Add flour, mace, and curry powder and cook 5 minutes more.

Add stock and simmer for 1 hour. Strain, rubbing solids through a sieve.

YIELD: 3 cups

Dill Sauce

    3 teaspoons lemon juice
    2 teaspoons grated onion
    3 tablespoons finely chopped fresh dill
    ½ teaspoon freshly ground black pepper
    1 ½ cups Mock Sour Cream (see page 206)

Blend and chill.

YIELD: 1 ¾ cups

Green Sauce

    1 cup Mock Sour Cream (see page 206)
    1 clove garlic, minced
    ¼ cup finely chopped chives
    ¼ cup chopped parsley
    2 tablespoons tarragon vinegar
    ½ teaspoon freshly ground black pepper

Blend all ingredients. Serve as a dip with crudités or with steamed vegetables.

YIELD: 1 ¾ cups

Horseradish Sauce

¼ cup finely grated fresh horseradish
1 cup Mock Sour Cream (see page 206)
¼ teaspoon freshly ground black pepper
1 tablespoon chopped parsley
Juice of ½ lemon

Combine all ingredients and chill.
Serve with raw vegetables.

YIELD: 1 ¼ cups

Horseradish Applesauce

½ cup freshly grated horseradish
2 cups homemade Applesauce (see page 212)

Mix to serve with steamed or baked potatoes.

YIELD: 2 ½ cups

Pesto

5 cups basil leaves, chopped
½ cup chopped parsley
½ teaspoon freshly ground black pepper
3 cloves garlic, crushed
½ cup Low-Fat Cottage Cheese (see page 203)
⅓ cup skim milk

Place ingredients in a blender or food processor and blend well.
Serve with pasta or rice.

YIELD: 3 cups

Tarragon Sauce

½ cup white wine vinegar
2 tablespoons finely chopped shallots
2 teaspoons dried tarragon
¼ teaspoon freshly ground white pepper
1 cup Low-Fat Cottage Cheese (see page 203)
½ cup skim milk

Combine vinegar, shallots, tarragon, and pepper in a saucepan; reduce liquid until vinegar is almost evaporated. Combine with cheese and skim milk in a blender and blend on high speed until mixture is smooth.
Serve with steamed vegetables.

YIELD: 2 cups

Tomato Sauce I

5 tablespoons Low-Fat Cottage Cheese
  (see page 203)
1 teaspoon mustard
1 teaspoon Worcestershire sauce
2 cloves garlic, mashed
2 tablespoons finely chopped parsley
2 tablespoons finely chopped fresh basil
½ teaspoon freshly ground black pepper
4 ripe tomatoes, diced

Combine cheese, mustard, Worcestershire sauce, garlic, parsley, basil, and pepper and mix well. Stir in tomatoes. Heat gently to serve.

YIELD: 1¼ cups

Tomato Sauce II

⅓ cup finely chopped onion
2 cups finely diced ripe tomatoes
2 cloves garlic, mashed
1 tablespoon tomato paste
1 bay leaf
Pinch of saffron
¼ teaspoon basil
½ teaspoon freshly ground black pepper
Vegetable Stock as needed (see page 47)

Heat ¼ cup water in a saucepan. Add onions and cook until soft. Add other ingredients and cook gently for 20 minutes, adding stock if necessary to prevent scorching. Remove bay leaf and purée sauce.

YIELD: 2½ cups

SALADS

Percy Bysshe Shelley wrote odes — and he also wrote a treatise in 1813 proposing that man was meant to consume only plants. Percy's theory remains a point of controversy. Be that as it may, other persistent vegetarians through the ages have included George Bernard Shaw, Dr. Dolittle, Yehudi Menuhin, Adam, Hindus, Trappist monks, Leo Tolstoy, Seventh Day Adventists, Isaac Bashevis Singer, Gloria Swanson, and Bugs Bunny. They would all enjoy these salads.

Artichoke Salad

9 young artichokes, leaves and chokes removed
Juice of ½ lemon
1 cup green beans, trimmed
3 red potatoes
1 green pepper, seeded and cut into strips
1 red pepper, seeded and cut into strips
2 ripe tomatoes, quartered
2 tablespoons chopped parsley
1 tablespoon chopped fresh basil
1 clove garlic, mashed
¼ cup cold Vegetable Stock (see page 47)
¼ cup tarragon vinegar
¼ teaspoon freshly ground black pepper

Paint the artichoke hearts with lemon juice and steam them for 15 minutes. Quarter them.
Steam the green beans for 8 minutes.
Boil the potatoes in water to cover for 30 minutes, or until just tender. Peel and quarter them.
Combine all the ingredients, mix well, and chill.

SERVES 6

Arugula and Celery-Root Salad

2 celery roots (celeriac), trimmed and washed
2 bunches arugula, torn into bite-size pieces
1 clove garlic, minced
1 teaspoon grated lemon peel
1 tablespoon chopped chives
Dill Dressing (see page 198)

Slice the celery roots thin, then cut them into strips.
Toss all the ingredients and serve.

SERVES 6

Mixed Bean Salad

½ cup each dried Great Northern beans, kidney
  beans, and chickpeas
1 clove garlic, mashed
½ cup finely chopped scallions
3 tablespoons finely chopped parsley
½ teaspoon Dijon mustard
2 tablespoons red wine vinegar
½ teaspoon freshly ground black pepper

*Place the beans and chickpeas in a pot with water
to cover and bring to a boil. Continue cooking them for
2 minutes, then cover and let them stand for 1 hour.
Simmer them until tender, then drain.*
*Combine all ingredients and toss well. Chill for 1 hour,
toss again, and serve.*

SERVES 6

Carrot Salad

1 ½ pounds carrots, peeled and coarsely grated
2 ribs celery, cut into small dice
1 tart apple, cut into small dice and tossed with
  lemon juice
½ cup Low-Fat Yogurt (see page 207)
¼ cup unsweetened apple juice concentrate
Freshly ground black pepper
Lettuce leaves (for garnish)

Toss carrots, celery, and apple together.
Blend yogurt, apple juice concentrate, and pepper and mix
with salad.
Serve on lettuce leaves.

SERVES 6

Chickpea Salad

1 cup dried chickpeas
¼ cup chopped sweet red pepper
¼ cup chopped parsley
2 ripe tomatoes, cut in wedges
½ cup Low-Fat Yogurt (see page 207)
½ teaspoon freshly ground black pepper
¼ teaspoon paprika
2 teaspoons lemon juice
Lettuce leaves (for garnish)

Place the chickpeas in a pot with water to cover and bring to a boil. Continue cooking them for 2 minutes, then cover and let them stand for 1 hour. Simmer until tender, then drain and chill them.

Combine chickpeas, red pepper, parsley, and tomatoes in a bowl.

Combine yogurt, pepper, paprika, and lemon juice and blend well. Add to chickpeas and toss lightly.

Serve on lettuce leaves.

SERVES 6

Chicory and Endive Salad

½ clove garlic, mashed
1 tablespoon white wine vinegar
2 tablespoons Mock Sour Cream (see page 206)
1 teaspoon dried tarragon
Freshly ground black pepper
1 head chicory, cut into bite-size pieces
3 Belgian endives, halved lengthwise
Whites of 2 hard-cooked eggs, diced

Blend garlic, vinegar, sour cream, tarragon, and pepper. Toss with chicory, endives, and egg whites.

SERVES 6

Coleslaw

1 firm head cabbage
3 carrots, shredded
1 small onion, finely chopped
Freshly ground white pepper
3 tablespoons lemon juice
½ cup Mock Sour Cream (see page 206)
2 teaspoons caraway seeds

Remove outer leaves from cabbage, cut in half, and remove core. Shred cabbage.
Mix all ingredients well and chill.

SERVES 6

Cucumber Salad

½ cup Low-Fat Yogurt (see page 207)
½ cup fresh dill
2 tablespoons lemon juice
¼ teaspoon mustard
¼ teaspoon freshly ground black pepper
6 cucumbers, peeled and sliced
6 Romaine lettuce leaves (for garnish)

Combine yogurt, dill, lemon juice, mustard, and pepper and chill. Combine with cucumbers just before serving.
Serve on lettuce leaves.

SERVES 6

Fennel Salad

2 large fennel bulbs, thinly sliced
½ pound mushrooms, thinly sliced
1 sweet red pepper, seeded and cut into thin strips
2 tablespoons minced scallions
Fresh Mint Dressing (see page 200)
6 large Boston lettuce leaves

Toss the fennel, mushrooms, red pepper, and scallions together with the dressing.
Serve in individual portions on the lettuce leaves.

SERVES 6

Green Bean Salad

2 pounds green beans
¼ teaspoon freshly ground black pepper
3 tablespoons lemon juice
1 clove garlic, mashed
½ cup minced parsley

Cook beans in plenty of boiling water for 5 minutes. Drain and rinse thoroughly with cold water to stop cooking.
Mix pepper, lemon juice, and garlic. Sprinkle beans with parsley.
Toss everything together and serve.

SERVES 6

Harvard Salad

2 potatoes, boiled and peeled
2 beets, cooked and peeled
2 McIntosh apples, peeled and cored
Spicy Dressing (see page 201)

Cut the potatoes, beets, and apples into ½-inch dice.
Toss them with the dressing and serve.

SERVES 6

Lentil Salad

1 cup dried lentils, washed and drained
1 bay leaf
1 onion, stuck with 2 cloves
½ onion, minced
2 radishes, grated
¼ cup bean sprouts
2 tablespoons minced parsley
½ teaspoon freshly ground black pepper

Combine lentils, bay leaf, the onion stuck with cloves, and 3 cups water in a saucepan. Bring to a boil, then lower to a simmer, and cook 40 minutes.
Drain, discarding onion and bay leaf.
Allow lentils to cool. Add other ingredients and serve.

SERVES 6

Mushroom Salad

2 pounds mushrooms, cleaned, trimmed, and cut
    into wedges
Juice of 1 lemon and 2 limes
5 scallions, minced
2 green peppers, cut into tiny dice
¼ cup minced parsley
½ teaspoon freshly ground black pepper
Boston lettuce (for garnish)

*Combine all ingredients and chill. Serve on lettuce
leaves.*

SERVES 6

Onions and Oranges

2 large red onions, peeled and sliced into very thin
    rounds
Lemon juice
3 large navel oranges

*Place onion slices in a bowl and sprinkle gener-
ously with lemon juice. Set in refrigerator for 1 hour.*
*With a knife, peel oranges to the flesh, then slice into
¼-inch-thick rounds.*
*On serving platter, overlap alternating orange and onion
slices in a circular pattern.*

SERVES 6

Pinto Bean Salad

¾ pound dried pinto beans
4 scallions, finely chopped
2 cloves garlic, mashed
2 tablespoons red wine vinegar
1 teaspoon Dijon mustard
¼ teaspoon curry powder

Place the beans in a pot with water to cover and bring to a boil. Continue cooking them for 2 minutes, then cover and let stand for 1 hour. Simmer the beans until tender, then drain them.

Combine all the ingredients in a mixing bowl and mix them thoroughly.

Cover the bowl and refrigerate the salad overnight.

SERVES 6

Creamy Potato Salad

¼ cup Mock Sour Cream (see page 206)
¼ cup Low-Fat Yogurt (see page 207)
2 teaspoons chopped scallions
½ teaspoon freshly ground black pepper
4 cups boiled potatoes, peeled and diced
Lettuce leaves (for garnish)

Mix sour cream, yogurt, scallions, and pepper.
Toss with potatoes. Serve on lettuce leaves.

SERVES 6

French Potato Salad

2 pounds boiling potatoes
¼ cup red wine vinegar
¼ teaspoon freshly ground black pepper
¼ cup minced parsley
2 teaspoons mustard

Boil potatoes in plenty of water until just tender
(about 45 minutes). Drain and place in pan over medium
heat to dry.
Peel and slice into ¼-inch slices.
Add vinegar immediately, while still hot. Mix in pepper,
parsley, and mustard. Serve warm or cold.

SERVES 6

Pseudo-Caesar Salad

1 clove garlic, halved
½ teaspoon mustard
2 tablespoons lemon juice
½ teaspoon freshly ground black pepper
3 tablespoons Mock Sour Cream (see page 206)
2 large heads Romaine lettuce, washed and torn
   into bite-size pieces
½ cup whole-wheat Croutons (see page 140)

Rub salad bowl with cut sides of garlic. Mix mustard, lemon juice, pepper, and sour cream in bottom of bowl.
Add lettuce and toss.
Sprinkle on croutons, toss, and serve.

SERVES 6

Rose Hill Salad

    1 clove garlic, halved
    3 heads Bibb lettuce, cut into bite-size pieces
    1 fennel bulb, sliced thin
    Whites of 3 hard-cooked eggs, chopped
    1 tablespoon lemon juice
    1 teaspoon mustard
    3 tablespoons Low-Fat Yogurt (see page 207)
    ¼ teaspoon freshly ground black pepper

Rub salad bowl with cut sides of garlic. Add lettuce, fennel, and egg whites.
Stir lemon juice, mustard, yogurt, and pepper together.
Toss with salad.

SERVES 6

Spinach Salad

      1 pound raw spinach, washed well
      1 clove garlic, minced
      Whites of 3 hard-cooked eggs, chopped
      18 cherry tomatoes
      1 small red onion, sliced thin
      Parsley Dressing (see page 201)

Tear off the tough stems of the spinach, then tear the leaves into bite-size pieces.
Combine all ingredients and toss well.

SERVES 6

Tomatoes with Basil

      6 large ripe tomatoes, sliced
      6 Romaine lettuce leaves
      ¼ cup roughly chopped fresh basil
      ¼ teaspoon freshly ground black pepper
      2 tablespoons red wine vinegar

Arrange the tomatoes on the lettuce leaves, 1 tomato per leaf. Sprinkle the tomatoes, first with basil, then with pepper, then with vinegar. Serve.

SERVES 6

Tomato-Potato Salad

2 ripe tomatoes
2 potatoes, boiled and peeled
1 rib celery
1 small red onion, peeled
2 tablespoons fresh chopped basil
Tarragon Dressing (see page 201)

Cut the tomatoes into wedges and the potatoes into ½-inch dice.
Slice the celery thin, horizontally.
Cut the red onion into thin rings and then toss all the ingredients together.

SERVES 6

Cherry Tomatoes with Chive Dressing

½ cup Mock Sour Cream (see page 206)
2 scallions (white part only), finely chopped
3 tablespoons finely chopped fresh chives
2 tablespoons lemon juice
¼ teaspoon freshly ground white pepper
2 pints cherry tomatoes, washed and trimmed

Combine the sour cream, scallions, chives, lemon juice, and pepper and mix well.
Toss with the tomatoes and serve.

SERVES 6

Waldorf Salad

2 apples, peeled and cored
1 celery root (celeriac), peeled
½ cup peeled, roasted chestnuts
2 ripe tomatoes, cut into wedges
Apple Dressing (see page 198)

Cut the apples and celery root into ½-inch dice. Toss all the ingredients together and serve.

SERVES 6

Watercress Salad

2 bunches watercress
7 Jerusalem artichokes, peeled and sliced
2 ripe tomatoes, cut into wedges
2 teaspoons minced scallions
¼ teaspoon freshly ground black pepper
2 tablespoons lemon juice

Cut the toughest stems off the watercress. Toss all ingredients together and serve.

SERVES 6

194.

Zucchini Salad

8 medium zucchini
5 tablespoons lemon juice
1½ teaspoons mustard
2 small cloves garlic, mashed
4 tablespoons Low-Fat Yogurt (see page 207)
¼ teaspoon freshly ground black pepper
1 medium red onion, finely chopped
5 tablespoons finely grated radishes
1½ tablespoons finely chopped parsley or
    fresh basil

*Cook zucchini 4 to 5 minutes in plenty of boiling
water. Drain and slice into ¼-inch rounds. Sprinkle with
2 tablespoons lemon juice.*

*Blend mustard, garlic, yogurt, pepper, and the rest of the
lemon juice. Pour over zucchini.*

Add onion, radishes, and parsley and toss well.

Chill and serve.

SERVES 6

DRESSING AND DIPS

Here are some exquisite dressings for salads and vegetables and some dips for dipping raw vegetables and toasted pita bread into. For those who prefer the simplicity of vinegar, however, let us mention that on a recent visit to a food emporium in New York, we discovered these vinegars: shallot, strawberry, raspberry, whortleberry, thyme, tarragon, cherry, red currant, cider with or without honey, lavender, *herbes de Provence*, green pepper, garlic, sage, clove, muscatel, nutmeg, rice, and, of course good old red or white wine. That very evening Ellen served green pepper vinegar on her baked potatoes and raspberry on her lettuce. No one missed butter or oil, and everyone was happy.

Apple Dressing

½ cup Low-Fat Yogurt (see page 207)
¼ cup apple juice concentrate
1 tablespoon lemon juice
1 tablespoon finely chopped parsley
¼ teaspoon freshly ground black pepper

Combine the yogurt, apple juice concentrate, and lemon juice and mix them well.
Add the parsley and pepper, stir well, and serve.

YIELD: 1 cup

Dill Dressing

½ cup Mock Sour Cream (see page 206)
½ cup Low-Fat Yogurt (see page 207)
1 tablespoon white wine vinegar
2 tablespoons lemon juice
¼ cup finely chopped fresh dill
½ teaspoon freshly ground black pepper

Mix all the ingredients and chill.

YIELD: 1¼ cups

Green Dressing

10 sprigs watercress
10 leaves fresh spinach
1 teaspoon finely chopped parsley
1 teaspoon dried tarragon
1 cup Low-Fat Yogurt (see page 207)
2 teaspoons lemon juice
¼ teaspoon freshly ground black pepper

Chop the watercress, spinach, and parsley very fine. Place them in a mortar with the tarragon and grind them to a paste.
Blend in the other ingredients.

YIELD: 1¼ cups

Herb Dressing

1 clove garlic, mashed
½ teaspoon dry mustard
1 teaspoon paprika
½ teaspoon freshly ground black pepper
½ teaspoon dried basil, crumbled
½ teaspoon dried tarragon, crumbled
⅓ cup white wine vinegar
½ cup chopped parsley

Combine all ingredients and shake well.

YIELD: ¾ cup

Horseradish Dressing

¾ cup Mock Sour Cream (see page 206)
3 tablespoons white wine vinegar
3 tablespoons grated horseradish
2 teaspoons finely chopped scallions
Freshly ground black pepper

Blend all ingredients well.

YIELD: 1 cup

Fresh Mint Dressing

¼ cup Low-Fat Yogurt (see page 207)
¼ cup Low-Fat Cottage Cheese (see page 203)
3 tablespoons lime juice
2 tablespoons chopped fresh mint
¼ teaspoon freshly ground black pepper

Blend the yogurt and cottage cheese until they form a smooth, creamy mixture.
Add the other ingredients and mix well.

YIELD: 1 cup

200.

Parsley Dressing

6 tablespoons Vegetable Stock (see page 47)
1 tablespoon red wine vinegar
2 tablespoons lemon juice
¼ cup chopped parsley
¼ teaspoon freshly ground black pepper

Combine all the ingredients and serve as a dip with crudités or with steamed vegetables.

YIELD: ¾ cup

Spicy Dressing

1 teaspoon Dijon mustard
6 tablespoons Low-Fat Cottage Cheese
  (see page 203)
3 tablespoons red wine vinegar
1 tablespoon soy sauce
1 teaspoon Vegetable Stock (see page 47)
1 teaspoon finely chopped parsley
¼ teaspoon freshly ground black pepper
2 dashes Tabasco

Beat the mustard into the cottage cheese. Add the vinegar, soy sauce, and stock and beat well.
Add the parsley, pepper, and Tabasco. Stir the dressing well and serve.

YIELD: ¾ cup

Tarragon Dressing

¼ cup Mock Sour Cream (see page 206)
2 tablespoons white wine vinegar
1 teaspoon Dijon mustard
1 teaspoon dried tarragon
¼ teaspoon freshly ground black pepper

Beat all the ingredients together and serve.

YIELD: ½ cup

Tomato Dressing

½ cup tomato purée
1 cup Low-Fat Cottage Cheese (see page 203)
¼ cup skim milk
2 tablespoons finely chopped onion
1 small green pepper, seeded and finely chopped
1 teaspoon chopped fresh chives

Blend the tomato purée, cottage cheese, and skim milk until they are smooth.
Pour the mixture into a bowl and stir in the other ingredients.

YIELD: 2 cups

Low-Fat Cottage Cheese

2 quarts skim milk at room temperature
¼ cup liquid rennet

Combine the milk with the rennet and heat it until it is very warm but not boiling (about the temperature of a good, hot bath).
Turn off the heat, cover the pan with a cloth, and leave the milk in a warm place overnight.
Pour the curds and whey into a piece of cheesecloth.
Tie the ends of the cloth together and suspend it over a basin for 15 to 24 hours, depending on how dry a cheese you want.

YIELD: 4 cups

Curry Dip

4 scallions, sliced very thin
2 teaspoons curry powder
¼ teaspoon ground cumin
2 dashes Tabasco
¾ cup Low-Fat Yogurt (see page 207)
¼ cup Mock Sour Cream (see page 206)

Cook the scallions with 2 tablespoons water until they become limp.
Add the curry, cumin, and Tabasco and cook gently for 3 minutes.
Combine the mixture with the yogurt and sour cream.
Chill.

YIELD: 1 cup

Dill Dip

1 cup Low-Fat Yogurt (see page 207)
1 tablespoon lemon juice
6 drops Tabasco
⅓ cup minced fresh dill
2 dashes Worcestershire sauce
¼ cup minced scallion

Combine all ingredients and chill.

YIELD: 1 ½ cups

Eggplant Dip

2 medium eggplants, halved
1 large onion, finely chopped
¼ teaspoon freshly ground black pepper
2 tablespoons finely chopped parsley
2 teaspoons lemon juice

Put the eggplant halves under the broiler, skin side up, until the skin is charred and peeling.
Scoop out the pulp and mince it very fine. Stir in the other ingredients. Chill.

YIELD: 2 ½ cups

Garlic Dip

¾ cup Low-Fat Yogurt (see page 207)
¼ cup Mock Sour Cream (see page 206)
2 cloves garlic, mashed
Juice of ½ lemon
¼ teaspoon freshly ground black pepper

Mix all ingredients and chill.

YIELD: 1 cup

Parsley Dip

1 cup Low-Fat Yogurt (see page 207)
½ cup finely chopped parsley
2 teaspoons vinegar
4 tablespoons grated radish
½ teaspoon freshly ground black pepper

Mix all ingredients and chill.

YIELD: 1 ¾ cups

Mock Sour Cream

1 can evaporated skim milk
2 teaspoons lemon juice
3 tablespoons Low-Fat Yogurt (see page 207)

Chill the milk for 12 hours. Place the milk in a chilled bowl, add the lemon juice, and beat it with a wire whisk until it thickens.
Fold in the yogurt.

YIELD: 2 cups

Low-Fat Yogurt

    1 quart skim milk
    2 tablespoons commercial low-fat yogurt

Bring the milk to a boil. Turn off the heat and allow it to cool to 110°F.

Beat a few tablespoons of the milk into the yogurt.

Add the rest of the milk bit by bit, beating constantly.

Cover the bowl very tightly. Wrap it in a blanket and place it in a draft-free spot.

Let the yogurt sit between 5 and 10 hours before refrigerating it. The longer it sits, the thicker and more acid it will become.

YIELD: 1 quart

DESSERTS

Ah, sweet mystery of life: dessert. Even a diet as rigid as ours cannot stifle the desire for something sweet to end the meal. For us, it is fruit. What is forbidden elsewhere (if you follow the Koran, for example, you know it was a banana, and not an apple, in the Garden of Eden), is not, you will be pleased to find, forbidden here.

Baked Apples

6 baking apples, cored
6 tablespoons apple juice concentrate
¼ teaspoon ground clove
½ teaspoon ground cinnamon

Preheat oven to 350°F.
Place 1 tablespoon apple juice concentrate, mixed with clove and cinnamon, in the center of each apple.
Arrange the apples in a baking dish and add water to a depth of ½ inch.
Bake, basting frequently, for ½ hour.

SERVES 6

Apple Cookies

2 cups sifted unbleached all-purpose flour
½ teaspoon baking soda
1 teaspoon cinnamon
½ teaspoon nutmeg
½ teaspoon allspice
¼ teaspoon ground clove
1 cup chopped apple
¾ cup apple juice concentrate
3 egg whites

Preheat the oven to 375°F.
Mix the flour, baking soda, cinnamon, nutmeg, allspice, and ground clove.
Stir in the chopped apple and the apple juice concentrate.
Beat the egg whites to soft peaks.
Fold in the other ingredients.
Dust your hands with flour and form the dough into tablespoon-size cookies. Place them on a nonstick cookie sheet and bake for 10 to 12 minutes or until they are lightly browned.

YIELD: approximately 3 dozen cookies

Apple Mousse

1 teaspoon gelatin
¼ cup apple juice concentrate
3 cups Applesauce (see below)
½ teaspoon vanilla extract

Dissolve the gelatin in the apple juice concentrate.
Add the applesauce and vanilla and chill for 1 hour.
Beat the mixture with a wire whisk until it doubles in bulk.
Chill for 4 hours or more.

SERVES 6

Applesauce

6 medium-size McIntosh apples
¼ cup unsweetened apple juice concentrate
Nutmeg, cinnamon, mace, or ginger to taste

Pare the apples. Quarter and core them. Place them
in a saucepan with the concentrate, cover, and cook over
medium heat for 10 minutes.
Remove the cover, shake the pan, and cook until the sauce
is thick.
Flavor with nutmeg, cinnamon, mace, or ginger.

SERVES 6

Poached Bananas

6 firm bananas
¼ cup orange juice concentrate
1 cup dry white wine
1 stick cinnamon

Peel the bananas and set aside.
Combine the other ingredients with 1 cup water and bring to a boil. Simmer for 5 minutes.
Add the bananas to the liquid and cook at a bare simmer for 5 minutes.
Allow them to sit for 15 minutes in the liquid before serving.

SERVES 6

Banana Whip

       1 ½ tablespoons gelatin
       3 tablespoons orange juice concentrate
       ½ cup boiling water
       3 egg whites
       3 bananas, peeled and cut up

Put the gelatin and orange juice concentrate in a blender with boiling water and blend for 30 seconds.
Add the egg whites and blend for 15 seconds more.
Add the banana pieces, several at a time, while continuing to blend.
Chill in the refrigerator 4 to 5 hours before serving.

SERVES 6

Frozen Blueberry Mousse

       1 pint blueberries
       ¼ cup apple juice concentrate
       2 egg whites

Purée the berries with the apple juice concentrate.
Remove the mixture to a bowl.
Beat the egg whites until firm, then fold them carefully into the blueberry mixture.
Freeze the mousse until firm at the edges, then stir it and freeze until the entire mousse is firm.

SERVES 6

Blueberry Sauce

    1 cup blueberries
    1 teaspoon cornstarch
    1 teaspoon lemon juice

Combine blueberries with ¼ cup water and bring to a boil.
Dissolve the cornstarch in 1 tablespoon cold water and add it to the blueberries.
Cook, stirring, until the sauce clears. Add the lemon juice, stir, and serve on fruit.

YIELD: 1 cup

Cherry Sauce

    1 pound sweet cherries, pitted
    1 tablespoon cornstarch
    1 tablespoon lemon juice

Place cherries in a saucepan with ¼ cup water. Bring to a boil.
Blend cornstarch with ¼ cup cold water and add to cherries.
Cook, stirring, until clear. Add lemon juice.
Serve with fruit.

YIELD: 1 cup

Roasted Figs

12 ripe figs

Place figs on a spit and place about 6 inches from broiler. Cook 4 minutes per side.

SERVES 6

Indian Fruit Cup

1 ripe Persian melon
1 pint strawberries, hulled
1 cup seedless grapes
½ cup pomegranate seeds
2 tablespoons rose water
¼ cup orange juice concentrate

Cut the melon in half and remove the seeds. Use a melon baller to remove the flesh.
Wash the berries and drain.
Combine all the ingredients with ½ cup water and mix gently.

SERVES 6

216.

Mixed Fruit with Orange Juice

½ pint strawberries, washed and drained
½ pint blueberries, washed and drained
2 peaches, peeled, pitted, and sliced
¼ cup fresh orange juice

Mix all ingredients and chill.

SERVES 6

Poached Peaches

6 fresh peaches
¼ cup orange juice concentrate
2 strips orange peel

Peel and halve the peaches, removing the pits.
Combine the orange juice concentrate, orange peel, and
1 ½ cups water and bring to a boil.
Add the peaches and simmer gently until soft.

SERVES 6

Poached Pears with Raspberry Sauce

6 ripe pears, peeled
¼ cup apple juice concentrate
2 cloves
1 stick cinnamon
2 thin slices of lemon
1 slice of tangerine
6 cracked peppercorns
Raspberry Sauce (see page 219)

Preheat oven to 400°F.
Place the pears upright in a pot so that they fit tightly.
Add the apple juice concentrate, cloves, cinnamon, lemon, tangerine, and peppercorns, plus water to cover.
Cover and bring to a boil.
Place the pot in the oven for 2 hours.
Allow the pears to cool in their juice.
Serve with raspberry sauce.

Note: *If you have the patience, try taking the liquid in which the pears have been cooked and reducing it to a few tablespoons. Add this to the raspberry sauce for added flavor.*

SERVES 6

Raspberry Sauce

1 pint fresh raspberries
⅓ cup orange juice concentrate

Wash the berries in cold water, drain, and place them with the orange juice concentrate in a blender.
Blend for 1 minute and strain through a fine mesh strainer.
Serve over fresh strawberries, raspberries, or other fruit.

YIELD: 1 ½ cups

Stewed Rhubarb

1 ½ pounds rhubarb
½ cup orange juice concentrate
1 strip of orange peel

Cut the rhubarb into 1-inch pieces.
In a saucepan, combine it with the orange juice concentrate, orange peel, and 3 tablespoons water. Cover and cook gently for 20 minutes, or until the rhubarb is just tender.
Serve warm or cold.

SERVES 6

Frozen Strawberry Mousse

1 quart sweet ripe strawberries, washed and hulled
¼ cup orange juice concentrate
3 egg whites

Place the berries and orange juice concentrate in a blender and blend until it makes a smooth mixture. Remove to a bowl.
Beat the egg whites until they form stiff peaks, then fold them carefully into the strawberry mixture.
Place the bowl in the freezer until the mousse is firm at the edges. Stir quickly, then freeze until the entire mousse is firm.

SERVES 6

Tropical Fruit Cup

1 pineapple, peeled and cubed
1 large orange, sectioned
1 ripe banana, peeled and sliced
1 pint strawberries, washed and hulled
¼ cup orange juice concentrate
2 thin slices of lemon
2 thin slices of tangerine

Combine the pineapple, orange, banana, and straw-berries and set aside.
Combine the orange juice concentrate, lemon, and tangerine with ¾ cup water and bring to a boil. Simmer gently for 5 minutes.
Turn off the flame and allow the liquid to cool.
Add it to the fruit and chill until ready to serve.

SERVES 6

Mint Drink

2 ½ cups water
A handful of fresh mint leaves (or 2 tablespoons
  dried mint)
3 ½ cups Low-Fat Yogurt (see page 207)

*Bring the water to a boil, pour it over the mint,
stir, and allow it to sit for 7 minutes.*
Remove the mint leaves and chill the water.
*Combine the flavored water and the yogurt in a blender,
briefly. Serve.*

YIELD: 6 cups

Homemade Tomato Juice

12 medium-size ripe tomatoes
Juice of ½ lemon
1 teaspoon freshly ground black pepper

Remove the cores from the tomatoes.
*Squeeze the tomatoes by hand, put them through a juicer,
or peel and purée them in a food processor.*
Add the lemon juice and pepper and refrigerate.

YIELD: 1 quart

SOME MENUS

We have, traditionally, plotted our meals the way we've been taught — well-balanced, which is to say meat, vegetable, and starch . . . or red, green, and white.

With this diet, however, traditional rules do not apply. It's time to rethink the menus, time to redecorate the plates. Vegetables and grains can vary greatly — in taste and texture as well as in color. And the fruits of the field are so much prettier than the stuff on the grocer's shelf.

Here are a few suggested menus. And they are only the beginning.

dry milk
apple juice   blend
cranberry
or
rasberries

french toast
little milk
little egg
little mash bananas
little vanilla or cinnamon

Lunch for a Winter's Day

    Minestrone
    Stuffed Manicotti
    Brussels Sprouts Purée
    Arugula and Celery-Root Salad
    Poached Peaches

Dinner in the Round

    Chickpea Soup
    Stuffed Green Peppers
    Potatoes with Garlic
    Baked Apples

An Elegant Lunch

    Watercress Soup
    Sweet Potato Soufflé
    Baked Endive
    Artichoke Salad
    Poached Pears with Raspberry Sauce

Dinner Espagnol

    Gazpacho
    Chili
    Spanish Rice
    Green Peas with Dill
    Mixed Fruit with Orange Juice

A Midsummer Night's Dinner

Steamed Artichokes with Lemon
Spaghetti Mentonnaise
Rose Hill Salad
Frozen Strawberry Mousse

Roman Holiday

Zucchini Salad
Pasta e Fagioli
Celery in Tomato Sauce
Cauliflower with Fennel
Roasted Figs

An Exotic Dinner

Cold Melon Soup
Oriental Lentils
Curried Brussels Sprouts
Cucumber Salad
Indian Fruit Cup

Luncheon in Green and White

Spinach Soup
Spaghetti with Fresh Herb Sauce
Steamed Cucumbers and Asparagus
Chicory and Endive Salad
Banana Whip

A Thanksgiving Dinner

Pumpkin Soup
Cabbage Stuffed with Chestnuts and Mushrooms
Green Beans with Mustard
Onions and Oranges
Apple Mousse

A Cocktail Party

Marinated Baby Carrots
Marinated Mushrooms
Pickled Cucumbers and Onions
Sweet Peppers à la Grecque
Watercress Sandwiches
Cucumber Tea Sandwiches
Baba Ghanouj
Hummus
Parsley Dip
Garlic Dip
Curry Dip

The Baba Ghanouj and Hummus can be used to make canapés or, like the dips, can be used with crudités.

A Buffet Dinner

Cucumbers à la Grecque
Eggplant Purée with raw vegetables

Gnocchi in Tomato Sauce
Stuffed Zucchini Boats
Ratatouille
Mixed Bean Salad

Apple Mousse

INDEX

Whole-wheat
  bread, 151
  pasta dough, 155

Y

Yogurt
  low-fat, 207
  soup, spinach-, 41
  spinach with, 105

Z

Zucchini
  boats, stuffed, 120
  grated, with fresh basil, 119
  salad, 195
  soup, 51
    Elizabeth's curried, 52

Date	Weight	Cholesterol

Date	Weight	Cholesterol

Date	Weight	Cholesterol

Date	Weight	Cholesterol